D1388394

HEART IN PILGRIMAGE

A Life of George Herbert

*Serving as an Introduction to
24 of his poems, with Commentaries.*

JANE FALLOON

Bloomington, IN  Milton Keynes, UK

authorHOUSE®

AuthorHouse™
1663 Liberty Drive, Suite 200
Bloomington, IN 47403
www.authorhouse.com
Phone: 1-800-839-8640

AuthorHouse™ UK Ltd.
500 Avebury Boulevard
Central Milton Keynes, MK9 2BE
www.authorhouse.co.uk
Phone: 08001974150

First published by AuthorHouse   2/22/2007

ISBN: 978-1-4259-7755-9 (sc)

Printed in the United States of America
Bloomington, Indiana

This book is printed on acid-free paper.

This book is dedicated
to
Dr. Rowan Williams,
The Archbishop of Canterbury,
whose great knowledge and love of the poetry of George Herbert
is an inspiration to Christians in the 21st century.

TABLE OF CONTENTS

FOREWORD

George Herbert - the name rings muffled bells in some people's minds. Wasn't he a contemporary of John Donne's? One of those metaphysical poets? And didn't we sing hymns at school that he had written? There was one that stuck in the memory about sweeping a room - unlikely line for a hymn? After that, vagueness creeps in. Did he write the line "I saw Eternity the other night" ? No, that was Henry Vaughan. What else *did* he write, and why should yet another book be written about him?

George Herbert deserves better than this. He deserves not only to have academics disagreeing about him, and having one book every ten years appearing about him, perhaps trying to prove which side of the great Protestant divide he supported, at a time just before King Charles I lost his head for seeming to be on the wrong side. Herbert is a major poet, and has been recognised as such by many great literary critics since his time. William Cowper in the 18th century found his poetry comforting at a time of great depression. Samuel Taylor Coleridge was the first serious critic in the 19th century to champion him. John Ruskin later declared him to be his favourite poet. T.S.Eliot and Seamus Heaney both wrote eulogistically of him in the 20th century, and many others have recognised and lauded his great worth. It is time he became part, again, of the consciousness of ordinary poetry readers in the English-speaking world - not only academics, but people who love to have, somewhere in their minds, a reservoir of perfect lines and verses they can summon up for their private delight when times are bleak or boring. Not many of us learn poetry by heart any more, either at school or later, but there are those of us who, if they have twenty minutes stuck in an unmoving tube train, or two hours waiting on a runway for a plane to take off, comfort themselves by saying over all the verses they can remember of Keats's Ode to a Nightingale, or their favourite Shakespeare sonnets for instance. They would find a great store of extra richness in Herbert. It would be infinitely well worth while to have some of them by heart, for those increasingly inevitable hours of frustration, when time seems to have utterly ceased to move .

People who love poetry have their favourite poets: Andrew Marvell, John Donne, W.B.Yeats, Gerard Manley Hopkins, Seamus Heaney. And yet probably there are only two or three poems of any of those poets that they can instantly bring to mind and quote . George Herbert left, at his death, a sequence of 184 poems. During a recent reading, straight through from beginning to end, I put stars against the ones that passed A.E.Housman's test for great poetry. Housman, in his essay 'The Name and Nature of Poetry' wrote:

> 'Experience has taught me, when I am shaving of a morning, to keep watch over my thoughts, because, if a line of poetry strays into my memory, my skin bristles so that the razor ceases to act.'

This sensation was talked about a few years ago as the tingle factor. I found that no fewer than thirty six of Herbert's poems created this sensation in me, and I put my stars against them. Thirty six poems out of 184 is an average of one in five: of how many other poets, apart from Shakespeare, could one say that thirty six of their poems create that feeling of wonder, delight, recognition of genius, sheer happiness and shock? In this book I shall include twenty four of those thirty six poems, and some of the comments on them by the academic writers I have been reading, as well as my own.

It was a rewarding exercise to read the collection, known now as 'The Temple' as an entity. T.S.Eliot wrote in the Spectator of March 12th,1932,

> 'Of all the 'metaphysical' poets, Herbert has suffered the most from being read only in anthologies.....yet, when we take Herbert's collected poems and read industriously through the volume we cannot help being astonished both at the considerable number of pieces which are as fine as those in any anthology, and at what we may consider the spiritual stamina of the work. Throughout there is brainwork, and

a very high level of intensity; his poetry is definitely an oeuvre, to be studied entire, and our gradual appreciation of the poetry gives us a new impression of the man.'

This is in an ideal world, where people have masses of time, and F.E. Hutchinson's Oxford edition of Herbert's work is still in print. Twenty four poems will, I hope, be enough to give an understanding and appreciation of his genius, without the need for The Temple to be read in its entirety, but perhaps they will inspire some people to wish to read his whole work for themselves.

Born in 1593, George Herbert was ten years old when the reign of Elizabeth Tudor ended with her death in 1603, and James VI and the Stuart dynasty came to the throne of England. His life, until his death just before his fortieth birthday in 1633, spanned years of comparative calm in the Church of England's history, after the previous century's turmoil. It is vital to see him against his historical and sociological background, but also to relate him to the start of the 21st century. There is a relevance in his life and poetry to our own time: a relevance that, once apprehended, can open doors to a new awareness of what it means to be a Christian.

Herbert's poems and writings are astonishing in their accessibility. Although he was writing nearly 400 years ago, his sentiments and humour are often amazingly modern and immediate: we are shaken to read turns of phrase and jokes that we can relate to with delight, and emotions expressed so honestly that we can instantly respond to them. We can revel in his witty use of words; his brilliant variety of metre; his felicity with rhymes. Most especially we can wonder at the depth of his need for God and his love for Christ, and his doubts as to his worthiness to be loved by them.

Even if Herbert hadn't written a line of poetry he would still be a person of absorbing interest. His family was distinguished: he had as friends and mentors some of the most influential people of his day. As well as John Donne and Francis Bacon, he had close ties with Bishop Lancelot Andrewes, who was responsible for the translation of the King James Authorised version of the Bible, and Archbishop William Laud. Nicholas Ferrar of Little Gidding was his good friend. For some years Herbert held the distinguished position of Orator to Cambridge University, which brought him into contact with King James and his court, and later with King Charles. The Earls of Pembroke were his cousins and friends.

Perhaps most interesting of all is his connection to the Church of England, at the stage of development it had reached during the brief three years at the end of his life when he was an ordained priest with his own parish near Salisbury. In 1630, when he was ordained, the factions of the church were starting to brew the grumbling dissensions, which erupted in the Civil War, in 1642, nine years after Herbert's death. Herbert straddled the middle way between those who were influenced by Calvin and the Puritans, and those who, like Lancelot Andrewes and William Laud, were influenced by the Arminian brand of theology. Had he lived beyond 1633, he might have become embroiled in these dissensions, which resulted in Laud's execution in 1645. Perhaps his humility and lack of political ambition would have saved him from becoming involved in the power politics which caused Laud to be beheaded. Herbert deliberately turned his back on the structures of worldly influence when he made his decision to become a priest.

Herbert was the first person to write a guide for Church of England clergy. He called it 'The Country Parson'. It is a work of thirty seven short chapters, giving his precepts on the ideal behaviour of a Church of England clergyman. To study this work is to realise that it embodies ideas that are now most vital and most pertinent to the Church of England. The precepts are not controversial. He was not basically interested in the politics of the theological questions of his day. One of his early poems, which he later left out of The Temple, was called 'The H.(oly) Communion'. In it he shows his lack of concern about one of the contentious issues of the time: consubstantiation versus transubstantiation: whether the sanctified bread at Communion contained within itself the body of Christ, or whether its substance actually changed into the body of Christ at the Communion table. Herbert wrote

> O Gratious Lord, how shall I know
> Whether in these gifts thou bee so
> As thou art evry-where;
> Or rather so, as thou alone
> Tak'st all thy Lodging, leaving none
> ffor thy poore creature there?

ffirst I am sure, whether bread stay
or whether Bread doe fly away
Concerneth bread, not mee.
But that both thou and all thy traine
Bee there, to thy truth, and my gaine,
Concerneth mee and Thee.

These are the first two verses of an eight-verse poem, which goes on in the same mocking vein. The most important and serious line is the last: 'My God, give mee all Thee'. Perhaps he thought the poem too frivolous for his final collection: it certainly shows his sense of fun, and his unwillingness to become involved in issues that he found unimportant to his own faith.

It will be important to try to discover in detail what the influences were that persuaded Herbert to become a parson at the end of his short life. His mother; John Donne; Lancelot Andrewes, who was dean of Westminster when Herbert first arrived at Westminster School and whose presence in his life continued when Herbert went up to Cambridge when he was sixteen; all these people must have had a bearing on the ultimate direction of his life . Nicholas Ferrar, the saintly founder of the community at Little Gidding must certainly have influenced him. They were, uncharacteristically, both members of parliament at the same time in 1624-1625. Ferrar was the person to whom Herbert, just before he died, sent the manuscript of his poems and Ferrar was responsible for getting them published.

Wordsworth, in his sonnet to John Milton, wrote 'England hath need of thee'. Now, it seems to me, England has need of George Herbert. His comprehension of what it means to be a Christian; his awareness of his own inadequacy and failures; his ability to express these beliefs, alternating with self-doubt, make a strong impact on anyone longing for a certainty of belief themselves. It is all too easy, in these cynical times, to dismiss religious beliefs as a lot of nonsense. Empiricist philosophers believe only what can be proved, and are contemptuous of those who have a need for faith in something beyond reason or experience. The element they leave out is the need humankind has for belief in an ultimate power of goodness - something higher, greater, wiser, more loving and forgiving than themselves. Because it is impossible to know for certain that such an entity as God exists, people turn to the mystics and poets of every age and religion: to artists who have their own apprehension of divinity, and can express their perceptions in ways that are understood by ordinary people. Herbert had this gift.

Such faith, although without reason or logic to support it, and in face of intellectual questioning, can't be dismissed as stupidity. Perhaps Herbert's best known lines are

> Let all the world in ev'ry corner sing,
> My God and King.

It is this total commitment, together with his quirkish sense of humour and sweetness that capture us. His questioning and doubts, when they come, endear him to us, and the way he resolves them comforts us. He is worth reading and knowing by heart because his humanity shines through every line. There is such variety, wit and charm in the poems that through his writing he appears to us a most delightful character himself: someone we are glad to have as an integral part of our lives.

Chapter One
FAMILY AND CHILDHOOD

George Herbert was the seventh child in a family of ten. He was born on April 3rd, 1593, in the county of Montgomery, in Wales. At the time of his birth his eldest brother Edward, who later became the First Lord Herbert of Chirbury, was eleven; Elizabeth and Margaret, his oldest sisters, were ten and eight, and his next oldest brothers, Richard, William and Charles, were six, four, and one. After his birth three more children were born: Henry, Frances, and Thomas - the last was born seven months after the death of his father Richard, who died in 1596, when George was three. Magdalene Herbert, George's mother, used to say that she had the same family as Job: seven sons and three daughters.

The Herberts were a distinguished family in Wales. The family descended from 'Herbertus Camerarius', who came over from France with William the Conqueror. Seven or eight generations later the Herberts became Earls of Powis, Lords Herbert of Cherbury and formed several untitled branches in Wales and in Ireland. Sir William Herbert of Raglan Castle, Monmouth, was knighted in 1415 by Henry V for his valour in the French wars. His descendants were Earls of Pembroke and Huntingdon. William Herbert, the first Earl of Pembroke, from Raglan Castle, was beheaded during the Wars of the Roses in 1469 at the battle of Edgecote, and his younger brother Sir Richard Herbert, met the same fate at the same battle. The Earl was buried at Tintern Abbey. The two Welsh branches of the Herbert family descended from these two brothers. George Herbert's great-grandfather was a nephew of that first Earl of Pembroke, being the son of the beheaded younger brother Richard.

George's oldest brother Edward later united these two branches of the Herbert family by marrying, when he was fifteen, his cousin, Mary Herbert, the daughter of Sir William Herbert. She was six years older than he was, but was to inherit great wealth from her father on the condition that she married a Herbert.

George's great-grandfather Richard and his son Edward lived in Montgomery Castle. But George was not born there. His grandfather Edward built for himself a fine house beside the castle known as Black Hall, and Richard, George's father, moved there before George was born, and brought up his family there, until his death in 1596. Richard was a handsome dark-haired man, courageous and well liked in the county. But three years before his death he was involved in a fracas in which he was severely wounded in the head - "his skull was cutt through to the Pia Mater of his brain" (Edward's autobiography) and this may have contributed to his early death. He had fathered ten children in fifteen years of marriage. His wife Magdalene was the daughter of Sir Richard Newport, who was descended from a Welsh hero with the redoubtable name of Wenwynwyn. She was left to bring up their ten children by herself, and she took them to stay for a few years with her widowed mother Lady Newport, at Eyton upon Severn. They stayed there until her mother's death in 1599. George's father had died intestate, and Edward, his oldest son, who was almost fifteen, obtained Wardship of the family estate - and married his cousin Mary shortly after his father's death.

The Earls of Pembroke played an important part in George Herbert's later life. William, third Earl of Pembroke (1580 -1630) was the Earl in residence at Wilton House, near Salisbury, when George took Holy Orders and became Rector of nearby Bemerton, but he died that same year. He was a patron of the Arts: Ben Jonson, Philip Massinger the playwright - who was the son of one of the Earl's retainers - and Inigo Jones benefited from his patronage. King James's company of actors, known as The King's Men, of whom Shakespeare was one, often performed for Pembroke (and the King) at Wilton. He was a Lord Chamberlain of the Court from 1615 -1630, and became Chancellor of Oxford University in 1617. Pembroke College Oxford was named after him. Some people believe that Shakespeare's 'W.H.', The Onlie Begetter of the sonnets, was William Herbert Earl of Pembroke. He was sixteen years younger than Shakespeare. His brother Philip inherited the title from him. Philip was only nine years older than George, and inherited the title just as George became Rector of Bemerton. He was called Philip after his uncle, Sir Philip Sidney, who was his mother Mary's brother. He had been created Earl of Montgomery in 1605, and his wife, Anne Clifford, became George's good friend, when they were living only a few miles apart, from 1630 to 1633.

Magdalene Herbert must have been a remarkable woman. After her mother's death she decided to move her large family, which included Edward's wife and later his babies, to Oxford, to make a home there for Edward who was an undergraduate at University College. Edward, in his autobiography, describes this period of their lives:

> "Not long after my marriage I went again to Oxford, together with my wife and mother, who took a house and lived for some certain time there: and now, having a due remedy for that lasciviousness to which youth is naturally inclined, I followed my book more closely than ever; in which course I continued till I attained about the age of eighteen, when my mother took a house in London, between which place and Montgomery Castle I passed my time, till I came to the age of one and twenty, having in that space divers children....."

Edward during these years was also renovating his ancestral home Montgomery Castle.

While living in Oxford, George started his formal education with tutors and schoolmasters. It was also during this time that his mother was said by his biographer Izaak Walton, to have first met the poet John Donne, who remained her friend and admirer all her life. He preached the sermon at her funeral, and dedicated various poems to her, including his 'Corona' sonnets, written between 1605 and 1609. He wrote her a verse letter in 1604, and a fine elegy 'The Autumnall'. They all show his respect and affection for her. She was possibly ten years older than he was, but a woman of great charm, intelligence and beauty, as the portrait, possibly by Sir William Segar, proves. The first lines of The Autumnall attest to Donnes's appreciation of her qualities:

"No spring nor summer, Beauty hath such grace
As I have seen in one autumnall face......
If 'twere a shame to love, here 'twere no shame,
Affection here takes reverence's name.
Were her first years the Golden Age; that's true,
But now she's gold oft tried, and ever new."

The portrait shows a woman dressed in a magnificently ornate ruff, with a jewelled head-dress and necklace of pearls: her hair is held back from her face in two high rolls; she has a high broad forehead, steadfast, intelligent eyes, and a humorous twist to her mouth. She has the look of someone who can organise, and who will stand no nonsense, but at the same time has understanding and warmth. She was without any doubt the first major influence on her young son George .

In 1625, a time of plague in London, Magdalene asked John Donne to stay with her in her house in Chelsea. By then his wife, whom he had married in 1601, had died, and Magdalene was married to her second husband, Sir John Danvers. The importance of Donne's influence on George Herbert as a poet, as a result of this close friendship with his mother, cannot be overestimated.

When Magdalene moved her family from Oxford to London in 1601 she found a house near Charing Cross, just beside the Strand. The Strand leads down, then as now, via Fleet Street, to St. Paul's Cathedral, which existed then in an earlier form, on the same site as Sir Christopher Wren's masterpiece, which was built after the earlier one was destroyed in the Great Fire of London, in 1666.

Donne speaks in his sermon at her funeral of "her fortune, her estate. Which was in a faire and noble proportion, derived from her first husband." Although with so large a household she had to watch her finances carefully, she was able to buy a house in the most sought after district of London. The Strand was where some of the richest men in England had their town houses. Lord Burghley, for instance, had a magnificent house with extensive gardens in the Strand, built in the 1570s. Its plan, lately discovered at Burghley House in Lincolnshire, is described as "the most complete representation of any of the great sixteenth century Strand palaces and gardens, built strategically between Westminster and the City by the greatest men of the Elizabethan period." (Country Life: March 23rd 2000. Paula Henderson and Jill Hussey.) Donne himself lived in the Strand in 1612, with his benefactor, Sir Robert Drury, and as Magdalene had her house there until 1618 and possibly longer, they would have been near neighbours. Her house must have been a large one, to house her family and servants, and as she was able to keep pigs and poultry, and a spring garden, she must have had quite extensive grounds as well. It is hard to picture a house like this so near to the Charing Cross district we now know, and we don't know whether her house was beside the river, but if it was, it was in a splendid position, with all the interest of the bustling river traffic for the children to watch from their garden.

It was a practical place to live, with six young sons still to be educated, because it was within easy walking distance of Westminster School, which at the beginning of the seventeenth century was one of the finest schools in England. It was only necessary to walk down past the Palace of Whitehall, where King James I held his court, to the school which was just beside Westminster Abbey and the Houses of Parliament. She had placed herself and her family in the midst of the most powerful seats of influence in the country. And she herself, again according to Donne, had at Oxford "contracted a friendship with divers reverend persons, of eminency and estimation." These friendships surely followed her to London. Magdalene was able to rear all of her ten children through childhood to adulthood: this was a remarkable achievement at a time when infant mortality was so prolific, and the plague a common happening in London.

Magdalene carried on her husband's family tradition of great hospitality, in her London house. Recently a 'Kitchen Booke' kept by her steward John Gorse, has come to light, in Powys Castle. In it he recorded, for several months of the year 1601, when George was eight, the people who came to stay and to dine with Magdalene Herbert, and what they ate. There were continual parties of twenty eight to twenty nine people. (Including servants, there were twenty six people permanently living in the house. This number included four nurses and chambermaids, ten servingmen, Edward's wife Mary, a nephew, a young friend, and eight of Magdalene's children: two of the boys were living in the country when Magdalene wrote out this list at the beginning of John Gorse's book.)

Distinguished musicians were often in the house. William Byrd was there for three meals between 14th and 25th June, 1601. He was at that time Organist of the Chapel Royal, appointed by Queen Elizabeth. The Chapel Royal is just beside Charing Cross, so it was simple for him to drop in on the Herbert family. John Bull, who was also at some point Organist of the Chapel Royal, had several suppers with the Herberts between April and May of that year (at the first of which a swan pie was cut.) George and his brother Edward were both accomplished lutenists, and George also played the viol. There is no doubt that his mother's guests were another great and lasting influence on him, and music was always a most important part of his life.

At night, so Donne reported, Magdalene "shut up the house with a cheerful singing of psalms". He also said of her : "She came to this place, God's house of prayer, duly not only every Sabbath but even in weekdays...... and as she ever hastened her family, and her company hither, with that cheerful provocation, "For God's sake let's go, for God's sake let's be there at the Confession!'" So, at this early age, George was exposed to his mother's enthusiasms, and, perhaps without him consciously realising what was happening to him, they became absorbed into his system.

George is thought to have entered Westminster school as a day boy in 1604, when he was eleven. His sponsor was probably the great Lancelot Andrewes, who was then Dean of Westminster, and a good friend of the family. He must have been yet another powerful influence on his life, perhaps in the end the strongest of all, both at school, and later at Cambridge, and until his death in 1625, eight years before George himself died.

To Lancelot Andrewes we are indebted for the Authorised Version of the Bible. He was its General Editor when it was published in 1611. His learning was admired by King James "above all his chaplains; and that king, being of most excellent learning himself could the better discover what was Eminent in another." (John Hacket: contemporary at Westminster of George Herbert.) Hacket goes on: "Indeed he was the most Apostolical and Primitive-like Divine, in my opinion....I am transported even as in a Rapture to make this Digression: for who could come near the Shrine of such a Saint, and not offer up a few Grains of Glory upon it ? Or how durst I omit it? For he was the first that planted me in my tender studies, and watered them continually with his

Bounty." T.S. Eliot thought his sermons "ranked with the finest English prose of their time." He left Westminster in 1605, but it is thought that George Herbert would have been there with him for one year, as a day boy, before he was promoted to being a King's scholar in 1605. There were forty scholars in the school, who were elected from boys who had already been in the school for one year. Lancelot Andrewes was one of the electors of King's Scholars to Westminster, and would have been responsible for electing George Herbert, just before he left to become Bishop of Chichester, in October 1605.

It is interesting to read a more detailed account of Lancelot Andrewes's influence on the scholars at Westminster. This comes again from John Hacket, and is what he told a later Dean of Westminster, John Williams, about his predecessor:

> "I told him how strict that excellent Man was, to charge our Masters, that they should give us Lessons out of none but the most Classical Authors; that he did often supply the place of Head School-master and Usher for the space of an whole week together, and gave us not an hour of loitering-time from morning to night. How he caused Exercises in Prose and Verse to be brought to him, to examine our Style and Proficiency. That he never walked to Cheswick for his Recreation, without a brace of this young Fry; and in that way-faring Leisure, had a singular dexterity to fill those narrow Vessels with a Funnel. And, which was the greatest burden of his Toil, sometimes thrice in a week, sometimes oftner, he sent for the uppermost Scholars to his lodgings at night, and kept them with him from eight till eleven, unfolding to them the best Rudiments of the Greek tongue, and the elements of the Hebrew Grammar, and all this he did to boys without any compulsion of Correction; nay, I never heard him utter so much as a word of Austerity among us."

From this panegyric we realise that Lancelot Andrewes was a truly vocational teacher. In 1580 he had been appointed Master of Pembroke Hall Cambridge, and through this connection would have been able to keep in touch with Herbert when he arrived in Cambridge after leaving Westminster.

The headmaster of Westminster in Herbert's time there was Richard Ireland, who was appointed to succeed William Camden, who was headmaster when Ben Jonson was in the school, in 1598. Jonson wrote of Camden:

> Camden, most reverend head, to whom I owe
> All that I am in Arts; all that I know.

Richard Ireland was said to 'have left little mark on the school.' he remained there until Dr. John Wilson was appointed in 1610, just after Herbert had left. Nevertheless, Ireland did have the perspicuity to recognise that in George Herbert he had a boy of great promise. Thomas Plume, in his biography of John Hacket, reported that Master Ireland said to Hacket and George Herbert, who went together to Trinity College Cambridge, "that he expected to have credit by them two at the University, or would never hope for it after by any while he lived: and added withal, that he need give them no counsel to follow their books, but rather to study moderately, and use exercise; their parts being so good, that if they were careful not to impair their health with too much study, they would not fail to arrive at the top of learning in any Art or Science."

The main subjects taught at Westminster were Grammar, Logic, Rhetorick, taught through translation and re-translation of Latin texts, and Greek from the fourth form. Music was taught for an hour on Wednesday afternoons, and again on Friday afternoon. When George was elected a Scholar in 1605, he would probably have become a boarder, living with the thirty nine other scholars in the Scholars' Chamber, which stood in Dean's Yard, and had formerly been the granary of the original monks, when the school was a Benedictine monastery. The scholars had their meals (to the accompaniment of Bible reading) in the College Hall. Laurence E.Tanner, in his book *Westminster School* (pub. Country Life 1934) tells us that 'every winter they were supplied with liveries or gowns of "sadd newe color at 5s the yard" or of "London Russet," and these served as their outer coats.'

On 5th November, 1605, the new Dean, the replacement for Lancelot Andrewes, was installed. He was one Dr. Neale. But that was not the most momentous happening that day at Westminster.

George Herbert's oldest brother Edward was at that time a Member of Parliament for Merioneth. The night before, he had been warned in a dream not to go to parliament that day. As it transpired, he would have been safe enough, as Guy Fawkes and his fellow conspirators were discovered before they could carry out their dastardly plot. But it must have been a thrilling time for the little boys at Westminster. A contemporary of George's at the school, Edward Hawes, aged 16, wrote a poem of eighty stanzas on the Gunpowder Plot, calling it "Trayterous Percyes and Catesbys Prosopeia." William Camden, the former headmaster, also published a narrative of the trial of Guy Fawkes and the gunpowder plotters, in 1607. It was an event that must have left its mark on all the boys and masters who were at Westminster on that day, for the rest of their lives.

Chapter Two
CAMBRIDGE

George Herbert stayed at Westminster school until the summer of 1609, when he was sixteen. In May of that year he was named a Westminster Scholar for Trinity College Cambridge. Westminster had -and still has - a special relationship with Trinity Cambridge, and also with Christ Church Oxford. The Statutes of the school set up by its Foundress, Queen Elizabeth, ordained that there was to be an annual election of boys to scholarships at these two colleges. Queen Elizabeth had taken great interest in the school, but as she died in 1603 Herbert would only have been told about her many visits to the annual Latin Play, and to watch the boys at work. King James had become Founder on his accession to the throne, and continued the royal patronage and interest of his predecessor.

Another boy who gained a scholarship to Trinity at the same time as Herbert was John Hacket, seven months his senior and much later to become Bishop of Lincoln and then of Coventry. Herbert's and Hacket's names first appear as residents of Trinity in the autumn of 1609.

But before that happened, a momentous event had befallen the Herbert family. George's widowed mother Magdalene, in February 1609, had married again, and her new husband was a man young enough to be her son. He was born in 1588, and was therefore five years younger than Magdalene's oldest son Edward, and only five years older than George. He was Sir John Danvers, the younger brother of the Earl of Danby. At the time of their marriage he was, if the date of his birth is accurate, 21, and Magdalene probably somewhere between 42 and 45. He was the same age as her third son Richard. According to John Aubrey in his Brief Lives, his brother the Earl 'was greatly displeased with him for this disagreeable   match.' But Aubrey also adds 'He married her for love of her Witt.' Aubrey also tells us what a remarkably handsome young man he was. 'In his youth' he says,' his complexion was so exceeding beautiful and fine that.... his companion in his travels did say that the People would come after him in the street to admire him.' There is no doubt that he was also a young man of great courage, to marry someone so much older, with ten children; some of them still at school.

Sir John's great passion was creating Italianate gardens. He had bought a house in the village of Chelsea. Aubrey tells us it was 'in the very place where was the house of Sir Thomas More Ld Chancellor of England.' This may not be accurate, but it must have been near: it was on the river, and had a large and beautiful garden. There was a bowling green three chains in length (66 yards); many statues, urns, a boscage (wildernesse); 'stately great gravel walks' four yards wide; pavilions of brick, and ' firre trees and pine trees; shumacks - apples and pear trees.' This was the first of many great gardens he was to make during his lifetime. His friend Sir Francis Bacon (Lord Verulam) loved the garden, and was often there Aubrey again:

> "I remember Sir John Danvers told me, that his Lordship much delighted in his curious pretty garden at Chelsey, and as he was walking there one time he fell down in a dead sowne (swoon). My Lady Danvers rubbed his face, temples, etc., and gave him cordial water; as soon as he came to himself, sayde he, Madam, I am no good footman."

Bacon did not greatly admire Sir John's learning. Aubrey tells us:

> "Sir John told me that when his Lordship had wrote 'The History of Henry 7,' he sent the Manuscript copie to him to desire his opinion of it before 'twas printed. Qd. Sir John, Your Lordship knows that I am no Scholar. 'Tis no matter, said my Lord, I know what a Schollar can say; I would know what you can say. Sir John read it, and gave his opinion what he misliked..... which my Lord acknowledged to be true, and mended it; Why, said he, a Schollar never would have told me this."

Another friend of the Danvers, who enjoyed visiting their Chelsea house and garden, was John Donne. He took refuge there at the time of a plague in London in 1624, and commented that George was there at the same time.

From the time of his mother's marriage, George would have two houses in London to go to from his school and Cambridge. His mother kept her house in Charing Cross, but it is likely that the couple spent more time in the healthier environment of Chelsea. This house, with its own little chapel, and a drawing room 'whose floor is chequered like a chess board' would become a place that George would think of as his summer home.

George's relationship with his stepfather was good. There are several letters which show this. One written from Trinity Cambridge in 1617/18 thanks Sir John 'for the diversities of his favours' and professes 'that the same heart, which you have won long since, is still true to you, and hath nothing else to answer your infinite kindnesses, but a constancy of obedience.'

It is interesting to speculate on how long it took Sir John to win George's heart: a young man of sixteen to whom his mother was all-important must have been considerably shaken to find her in love with his brother's contemporary. He could well have been resentful and jealous. His oldest brother Edward significantly never said a word about his stepfather when he wrote his autobiography, even though Sir John worked valiantly, for years, on his behalf, helping to sort out his estate and his financial problems. Edward apparently did not welcome his stepfather into his family. But Sir John must have been a man of great charm. John Aubrey ends his account of him like this:

> Sir John, being my Relation and faithful Friend, was wont in fair mornings in the Summer to brush his Beaver-hatt with Hyssop and Thyme, which did perfume it with its natural Spirit, and would last a morning or longer.'

He was also deeply religious, and this must have been what cemented his long marriage to Magdalene, which lasted until her death in 1627 eighteen years later.

Meanwhile George, not yet seventeen, had arrived in Trinity College Cambridge with his friend John Hacket, in the autumn of 1609. He certainly must have shared Hacket's enthusiasm for Trinity. In Plume's biography of Hacket, he describes Hacket giving

> 'great thanks to God that he was not bred among rude and barborous people, but among civil and learned Athenians; that he was not disposed to some Monkish society, or ignorant Cloyster, but to the Greece of Greece itself, the most learned and Royal Society of Trinity College, which in that and all other Ages since the foundation equalled any other Colledge in Europe for plenty of incomparable Divines, Philosophers, and Orators.'

Trinity College in 1609 was one of the newer foundations among the Cambridge colleges. It was founded by Henry VIII, nearly at the end of his life, in 1546.He established it for a specific purpose; to produce future leaders for his newly reformed Church of England. In Herbert's time only two colleges were newer: Emmanuel was founded in 1584, and Sidney Sussex in 1596. There were thirteen other colleges in Cambridge at that time, making sixteen in all. The oldest was Peterhouse, founded in 1284; the three next oldest were Clare, founded in 1326, Pembroke, founded in 1346, and Gonville and Caius, founded in 1348. The other colleges then existing were Trinity Hall,1350, Corpus Christi 1352, Magdalene, 1428, King's, 1441,Queen's,1448,St. Catherine's, 1473, Jesus,1497, Christ's, 1505, and St. John's,1511. Now Cambridge University is made up of 31 colleges: the university is almost double the size it was then.

Although the foundation of Trinity as a college was comparatively new, the buildings it was housed in were two centuries older. There were two existing colleges on the site: King's Hall (nothing to do with King's College) which had received its charter in 1337, and Michaelhouse, an even earlier foundation, dating from 1327, and founded by Edward II's Chancellor of the Exchequer. These two buildings formed opposite ends - north and south respectively - of what is now Trinity's Great Court. When Herbert and Hacket arrived there, considerable building work was still in progress. Henry VIII had endowed the college with land and money derived from the dissolution of the monasteries, and the Master of Trinity, Thomas Nevile, who was appointed to the position by Queen Elizabeth in the year of George's birth, 1593, started that very year to direct the architectural development of the college. His work continued on until 1615, and in that time he had joined the existing structures of the earlier colleges to form the Great Court - building the dining hall where Michaelhouse had been, and creating an entirely new court between the Great Court and the river, which is called Nevile's Court after him. He funded its construction from his own pocket.

Eventually Trinity grew to become the largest of all the Cambridge colleges, but when Herbert arrived there this was not so. It would not have been much larger than the fifteen other colleges. It would be an interesting study to work out what Cambridge did consist of in Herbert's day: which familiar landmarks were already there, and which, such as the Senate House, Gibbs building beside King's College chapel - luckily Herbert knew this incomparable building and its wonderful windows - and the Wren Library in Trinity, did not yet exist. One certainty is that the proportion of women to men in the town would have been infinitesimal compared to today. Cambridge was a totally masculine university; no dons or fellows were allowed to be married, and the thought of women undergraduates was beyond anyone's wildest imaginings. Thomas Cranmer, when a fellow of Jesus College a hundred years earlier, had surreptitiously married, and when this was discovered he had to forfeit his fellowship. When his wife, and the child she bore him, died, he was allowed to be re-instated, and was later able to be ordained. Had she lived, the course of the Reformation might have been entirely different.

George Herbert had done exceptionally well to gain one of the only three Westminster scholarships to Trinity College Cambridge to be awarded in 1609, and he continued to achieve academic distinction at Cambridge. This is proved certain by the recorded fact in the Ordo Senioritatis of 1612, when he graduated to become Bachelor of Arts, that he was ranked second in the first twenty of the 193 B.A.s that year. When he became an M.A. three years later he was ranked 9th. He studied the Humanities and Liberal Arts, and became a proficient Latin and Greek scholar. Later in his Cambridge career, he studied Divinity. He quickly became a sublector, one of four who assisted a Head Lecturer for a one year term, in Greek, Latin, Mathematics, and Greek grammar. In 1618 he was appointed one of four 'Barnaby Lecturers' (appointed on June 6th: St Barnabus day). His appointment was to lecture in English on classical authors - particularly to first year undergraduates.

His public lectures on rhetoric were especially appreciated by an undergraduate at St. John's College, Symonds D'Ewes. He became a minor fellow in 1614, and a major fellow in 1615/6.

While he was at Cambridge he wrote ten of the nineteen of his letters which still exist. It is a tragedy that only this small number of his letters written in English remain: there are a few more written in Latin - notably one to Bishop Lancelot Andrewes - but the rest have been lost. Letters give such a clear impression of their writers' characters, and reading these few of Herbert's brings him vividly to life. Two were written to his mother, six to his stepfather Sir John Danvers, one to his sister Elizabeth, ten years his senior, and one to his brother Henry, fifteen months his junior.

His first letter to his mother - of which only a fragment remains - was written in 1609, at the end of his first term at Cambridge. He had been ill, and was to continue in bad health for the rest of his life. He tells her: ' I fear the heat of my late Ague hath dryed up those springs, by which scholars say, the Muses are to take up their habitations.' And this he is saying to excuse, humbly, the quality of the two sonnets he is sending her with the letter. They are not, certainly, great poetry, but they are important because they proclaim his decision that from then on any poetry he writes will never be love poetry, but will only be expressing his relationship with God. He tells his mother:

> 'My meaning(dear Mother) is in these sonnets, to declare
> my resolution to be, that my poor Abilities in Poetry, shall
> be all, and ever consecrated to God's glory. And...' (The rest
> of the letter is lost.)

The letter is especially interesting, because it shows that at the start of his life at Cambridge, he believed he would always be writing poetry. Even though none of his English poems appeared in print until after his death, he was already writing poetry at the early age of sixteen, and was certain that he would go on doing so. He knew, at that early age, that he was a poet. And he also knew that he had a vocation, to express his worship and praise of God through his poetry.

The next letter from Cambridge, to his stepfather, was written eight years later, in 1617. He must have written countless letters between this and the first one to his mother, but they are lost. By this date Herbert had become a Master of Arts and a major fellow at Trinity, and was lecturing on several different subjects. He was probably also tutoring several students in Trinity. Two of his brothers, William and Charles, had died. William, who was four years older than George, died fighting in the Low Countries in 1616 or 1617. Charles, one year older,and a fellow at New College Oxford, died in 1617, aged only 25. George's first letter to Sir John is a short one, simply thanking him, with affection and respect, for the gift of a horse. The second written not long after, is much more interesting, because in it Herbert wrote that he had decided to 'set foot into Divinity, to lay the platform of my future life.' It was written when he was 24. It is a letter which, as one reads it, brings him compellingly to life. It is written with some impatience; with a certain self-mockery,and with passion. He needs books - he must have books, he is frustrated without them, and he hasn't enough money to buy them for himself. Will his stepfather help him? One reason his annuity - £30 a year, granted him by his oldest brother Edward - doesn't stretch to books is because he has been ill, and his illness has been expensive: 'Infirmities are painful and costly.' He has to eat special food: 'I am fain to dyet in my chamber at mine own cost.' He does buy books, but : 'If a book of four or five shillings come in my way, I buy it, though I fast for it.' But to set foot into Divinity he needs: 'those infinite Volumes of Divinity which yet every day swell, and grow bigger.' He wants his stepfather to persuade his family (he writes of them as 'his friends') perhaps to allow him to use a future annuity; he doesn't want his stepfather to pay for the books.

His plea for books is heard. The next letter to Sir John, written in 1618, tells of a parcel of books his younger brother Henry has sent back from Paris. George knows that his stepfather has paid for them, but thinks that if his sister knows, she will re-imburse Sir John for at least five or six pounds, and he again suggests that his annuity should be doubled now 'upon condition that I should surcease from all title to it, after I entered into a Benefice' - i.e after he has entered the church. He wants to be independent, not always begging his family for money. If he had his own means he would 'for ever cease my clamorous and greedy bookish requests.' He says, with conviction: 'It is high time now that I should be no more a burden to you.'

The next surviving letter to Sir John is dated September 1619. It is full of suppressed excitement. He tells him he is 'to make an Oration to the whole University of an hour long in Latin'. The excitement is due to the possibility of his being given the post of orator to the university. the current orator was Sir Francis Nethersole, of whom Herbert says: 'He and I are ancient acquaintance.' Nethersole's influence would be important to Herbert in helping him to the oratorship. He asks Sir John to help him by sending Sir Francis a letter written by the Master of Trinity, John Nevile, which sets forth the University's (good) opinion of Herbert.But Herbert was already confident enough in Nethersole's opinion of him. He says: 'If you cannot send it with much convenience, it is no matter, for the Gentleman needs no incitation to love me.' He goes on to tell Sir John:

> 'The orator's place ......is the finest place in the University, though not the gainfullest; yet that will be about 30l. per an. but the commodiousness is beyond the Revenue; for the Orator writes all the University letters, makes all the Orations, be it to King, Prince, or whatever comes to the University, to requite thse pains, he takes place next the Doctors, is at all their Assemblies and Meetings, and sits above the Proctors, is Regent or non-Regent at his own pleasure, and such like Gaynesses, which will please a young man well.' (Herbert was 26 at this time.)

The next paragraph is so honest and charming. He is impatient to hear from Sir Francis, and then says:

> 'I hope I shall get this place without all your London helps, of which I am very proud, not but that I joy in your favours, but that you may see, that if all fail, yet I am able to stand on mine own legs.'

The next letter to Sir John is written the following month - October 6th, 1619. He has had the letter from Sir Francis Nethersole which he was waiting for, but it expresses doubts which we may all be having at this stage - if his future is to be Divinity, why is he attempting to gain this civil appointment which has nothing to do with the church? He writes:

'I understand Sir Francis Nethersole's Letter, that he fears I have not fully resolved of the matter, since this place being civil may divert me too much from Divinity, at which, not without cause, he thinks I aim; but I have wrote him back that this dignity, hath no such earthiness in it, but it may very well be joined with Heaven; or if it had to others, yet to me it should not, for aught I yet knew.'

If previous orators had been too much occupied with worldly things, that did not mean that he would be like them.

In this way Herbert justified his longing for this appointment so full of prestige and dignity - and so full of 'gaynesses', and which he knew would please him so well. He could still be 'laying the platform for his future life' in Divinity; he was convinced the oratorship would not be a side step from his ultimate destination in the church.

His great wish was granted: fifteen days after he wrote this letter, he was appointed deputy orator to Sir Francis Nethersole. And exactly three months later, on 21st January 1620, he was appointed university orator, at the age, still, of 26.

For the next four years George Herbert fulfilled his duties as university orator. During that time he had to deliver a farewell in Latin to King James I when he left Cambridge, and the same year - 1623 - an oration during the visit of Prince Charles (later Charles I). During that time, as well, he was seriously ill. In 1622 it was reported by Joseph Mead, of Christ's College, that 'Our Orator.... they say will not escape being at death's dore.' According to the Trinity college records he was absent from meals in hall at Trinity for twelve weeks. He spoke of his illness as 'the Ague'; posssibly it was a sort of rheumatoid arthritis - his eventual death was from consumption. His sister Elizabeth, who was married to Sir Henry Johnes of Carmathenshire, was also seriously ill at this time, and Hutchinson believes that she and George suffered from the same symptoms, and eventually died of the same disease. Elizabeth, according to her brother Edward, was seriously ill for a long time. 'For the space of about fourteen years she languished and pined away to skin and bones, and at last died in London.' But she outlived her brother George by a year. His brother Richard, six years older than him, died in

1622, and his sister Margaret, eight years older than him, and married to John Vaughan, another Welshman, died in 1623.

At the end of 1623 George Herbert was somewhat surprisingly elected to parliament, representing Montgomery borough. His friend Nicholas Ferrar was elected to parliament at the same time. Briefly they must have been members of parliament together. Their friendship must surely have begun in Cambridge, when Ferrar was both undergraduate and later fellow of Clare College, only a short walking distance from Trinity, during many of the years that George spent in Cambridge, and while members of parliament their friendship must have entered a new phase.

Ferrar's friendship with George Herbert is most important. He was a most remarkable and admirable man, and was ultimately responsible for the publication of Herbert's poetry.

In 1624, Herbert was ordained deacon. This was the first step needed before ordination as a priest in the church of England. It was something expected of fellows of Trinity who were M.A.s: they were all meant to be ordained Deacon seven years after they became Masters of Art. In Herbert's case it was eight years. This was a time of transition for Herbert, for from 1624 onwards, although he still held the post of orator, he left Cambridge and his academic life there, to spend more time in London with his family.

Chapter Three
NICHOLAS FERRAR

Nicholas Ferrar and George Herbert were contemporaries. Ferrar was born in February 1592, and Herbert in April 1593, so their births were separated by only fourteen months. Their social standing, so important at that time, was not quite the same: Ferrar wrote in his preface to Herbert's 'The Temple' that Herbert was 'nobly born'; he himself was the son of a wealthy London merchant, also called Nicholas, and his wife Mary, who came of a good county family, the Woodenoths of Cheshire. Nicholas Ferrar senior was an influential man, interested in overseas trade with the new colony of Virginia, and a friend of such seamen as Sir Francis Drake and Sir Walter Raleigh .He and his son John were involved in the Virginia Company, whose full name was 'The Treasurer and Company of Adventurers and Planters of the City of London for the first Colony of Virginia'. Later young Nicholas also became closely involved with this company. In looks he was reported to be 'small, fair-haired, precocious and frail'.* He was the youngest - but - one of a family of six. *(from intro. to Parl. papers of N.Ferrar by David R.Ransome, in R.H.S. Camden papers 5th series vol.7.)

Ferrar went up to Cambridge earlier than George Herbert; he became an undergraduate at Clare Hall in 1605, when he was only thirteen. Herbert did not arrive at Trinity College until 1609, when he was sixteen. But Ferrar stayed on for some years at Clare: in 1610 he gained his B.A. and became a Fellow of Clare - his subject was medicine - and he was still there in 1612, when, like Herbert, his health began to suffer. Cambridge was cold, damp, and windy, and both Ferrar and Herbert suffered from similar symptoms: ' agues and aguish distempers'. (John Ferrar). He was advised to travel abroad for his health, and left Cambridge that year to go as secretary to King James's daughter Elizabeth, when she travelled to Hanover to marry the Elector Palatine. In 1612 Herbert, then nineteen, graduated to become a B.A. He and Ferrar were both equally interested in religion, and this could have caused their paths to cross. They were also both top performers, of great academic distinction in their nearby colleges. It is unlikely that they did not at least each know of the other's growing reputation, even if they were not at this stage the friends they later became.

For some years after this, however, they went their separate ways. Ferrar travelled with Princess Elizabeth to Germany in 1613, and stayed on the Continent for another five years, not returning to England until 1618. Before he left London he wrote a valedictory note which he left for his parents to read after he had gone. He wrote:

> "O Lord, thou knowest I may truly say that from my youth up, thy terrors have I suffered with a troubled mind. My soul hath been almost rent, through violent temptations that have assaulted it."

Bernard Blackstone, who edited the Ferrar papers, (Cambridge U.P. 1938) says of this document that it was almost the only piece of self-revelation in his writings, and that he was prone to desolation and melancholy. He commented:

> "The restraint, the quiet dignity, and the objectivity of Ferrar's writings proceed rather from a continuous inner tension than from habitual serenity."

The same could be said of Herbert's poetry - which must be one reason why it appealed so strongly to Ferrar when he read it for the first time, after Herbert's death.

Ferrar spent time in Germany, Poland, France, Italy, and walked most of the way across Spain. On his travels he visited several monastic communities, and learnt how these gatherings of ascetic, sometimes hermitic, people lived. One such community that especially interested him was the Oratory of St. Philip Neri in Venice. Philip Neri lived from 1515 to 1595 and was canonised in 1622, not long after Ferrar visited the community he founded. Later, his settlement at Little Gidding demonstrated how much he had learnt from St. Philip Neri.

While he was in Madrid he heard, in a trance, that he was needed back in London to help his family, and especially his older brother John, out of their troubles. So he went back at once to England. His health was greatly improved by this time, and he would have liked ideally to go back to his academic life in Cambridge, but he realised that his family did need him, and he decided to stay with them in London. For the next few years his interests were all in London. He himself became a member of the Virginia Company, ending up as deputy to its governor, the Earl of Southampton. He also decided to stand for parliament, and became an MP in 1624, representing Lymington in Hampshire. George Herbert also became an MP in the parliament of 1623/24, representing the borough of Montgomery. It is certain to me that they were by then more than merely friends. Herbert's stepfather Sir John Danvers was an important member of the Virginia company, and Herbert was deeply concerned with the well-being and eventual fate of the company. Records show that he and Ferrar were actively participating as members of parliamentary committees during the same period: Ferrar was present, for instance, at a committee concerning freer fishing off the east coast of America, which he attended three times after its preliminary meeting on 15th March,1624; and Herbert was present, for instance, at a committee meeting concerning the estate of the Edwards family, in April 1624. The most important speech that Ferrar made was delivered to a committee concerned with the Virginia Company on 28th April 1624. They were both attending committee meetings in the same building at the same time. The House of Commons, then as now, was a sociable place, and they must have spent time there together. The reason this needs to be emphasised is because John Ferrar in his biography of Nicholas, has the sentence 'N.F. and Mr. Herbert, holding intercourse of letters, tho' otherwise very seldome (as I take it) having but once had personall Conference with each other'. This I feel sure must be inaccurate: so close a friendship as developed between them could not have grown from only one meeting.

The trouble afflicting the Ferrar family, which resulted in Nicholas staying in London to be with them, was caused by dishonest dealings being uncovered in the Virginia Company. The Lord Treasurer, the Earl of Middlesex, was charged with accepting 'bribes and other exorbitances'

(John Ferrar's Life of N.F.) He took the patent from the company 'under the pretence that it should ....yield a greater revenue to the king than it did'. Nicholas Ferrar was ordered, together with Lord Devonshire and Sir Edwin Sandys, to draw up a charge against him, which caused Nicholas to have to make the speech to the committee in the House of Commons which had to implicate the king in the fraudulent activity. The speech was well received, but Ferrar bitterly regretted having to make it. Jebb in his biography of Ferrar tells of his feelings;

> 'For these engagements and his too free speeches against the will of his Prince, though exceedingly well meant were so long a regret and shame to him afterwards, that he was heard to say (stretching out his right hand) "I would I were assured of the pardon of that sin, though on that condition this right hand were cut off."

He had all the court books and registers etc. of the company copied, foreseeing the storm and afraid they would be confiscated; and gave them to the Earl of Southampton. He also bailed his brother John out of his involvement with the company, with the loss to himself of £3,000. He did not remain in parliament for more than a year. Nor did George Herbert.

Alike in this, they were also alike in each deciding to become a deacon in the Church of England, within a year or two of each other. Herbert was made a deacon in 1624, and Ferrar in 1626. But before Ferrar took this step, he had taken an even more significant one: he had moved with his family to Little Gidding.

1625 was a year when plague hit London. Nicholas Ferrar realised he should move his widowed mother and the rest of her family to the country. The year before, she had bought the Lordship of a manor in Huntingdonshire (now in Cambridgeshire) called Little Gidding. It was a small property, consisting of a dilapidated manor house, a church which was being used as a barn, a pigeon house, and a small cottage. One of her daughters, Susanna, was married to a John Collett, and lived near Cambridge. The family moved in with her while they set about restoring the manor house and the church. Mrs. Ferrar refused to allow the house to be restored until the church was put in order, and so it was immediately most carefully furnished and 'was provided with everything necessary for that decency of divine worship which Laud was striving to introduce into the English church.'(D.N.B., Written by Mandell Creighton.) Gradually the rest of the property was restored, and they, together with the Collett family, and John Ferrar and his family, were able to move in that same year. It was here that the most important work of Nicholas Ferrar's life began.

Nicholas had determined to create a community which was founded in the Anglican faith, and would exemplify this by living a life consisting of prayer, service, and worship. Mandell Creighton in the D.N.B.explains it this way:

> 'Ferrar had seen enough of the world and its ways. He shrank from the struggle which he saw would soon break out between Charles I and parliament, and fell back upon an old design, of spending his days in religious retirement and the practice of devotion. He had been offered one of the greatest heiresses in London for a wife, but declined, saying that he had determined to live a single life. The animosities of public life caused him remorseful feelings, and he set to work to wind up his business concerns that he might withdraw from London.'

Bernard Blackstone in his edition of the Ferrar Papers (Cambridge 1938) further explains his convictions:

> 'The passion for holiness which in those early days drove courtier and cowherd alike into the desert, found its expression as much in a sweet charity as in bitter and unparalleled austerities; and the Christian doctrine that supernatural virtue does not destroy the warm and simple virtues of kindliness and friendship, but gives human nature its perfection, was never more clearly vindicated. This was the chief lesson which Nicholas Ferrar learned from his study of the ascetics, and it was upon the balance of human affection and superhuman charity that his community at Little Gidding rested.'

Blackstone added:

> 'An essential part of the lesson which Nicholas Ferrar learned
> from his hermits was the danger of unrelieved spirituality.
> What was dangerous for the solitary, indeed, would have
> been catastrophic for a community.'

Ferrar realised that what was needed was a judicious mixture of
activity and contemplation, and he set about devising a way of life and a
timetable to achieve this. He had a built-in community provided by his
family for a start. His mother was the most important person of course;
his sister and her husband John joined them with their numerous
children: fourteen in 1625 and eventually sixteen; his brother John
and his first wife Bathsheba were there working from the beginning,
and soon after, the rest of Nicholas's siblings - the ones that were still
living - joined their mother and her family. He already had about thirty
people, and gradually more would join them, to mould together into
the communal way of life that he had foreseen as the ideal existence
for a truly Christian society.

Before the enterprise was fully set in motion, Nicholas surprised the
world which he had left in London by becoming a deacon in the Church
of England. On Trinity Sunday, 1626, he went 'without acquainting any
of his friends'(John Ferrar) with his tutor from Clare, Dean Linsell, to
Westminster Chapel, and there Bishop Laud (later Archbishop Laud)
through the ceremony of laying on of hands, made him a deacon. It
astonished his friends and acquaintances in the court and the city that
he should take this step, especially Sir Edwin Sandys of the Virginia
Company, who was devoted to him. When it was realised that he was
set on a religious life several lords offered him a living in their parishes:
he refused them all. He had resolved, first, that he did not wish to take
any higher position in the church, and next, to spend the rest of his
life at Little Gidding.

So the great work of his life began. A modus vivendi was set up
for the community. The day began for them at 4.0 a.m. in the summer,
and 5.0 a.m. in the winter, and they went to bed at 8.0 p.m. in summer,
and 7.0 p.m. in winter. Although most of the day was organised into
set periods when they each worked at their allotted tasks, they also had
time for recreation, and this was provided by Nicholas's gift for story-

telling, and for encouraging others to tell stories as well. These were told or read at mealtimes - they were by no means always religious - there would be chronicles of nations, history, sometimes 'some easy and delightful matter'. It was the younger children who read - 'they first eat their broth, then read.' Then a summary of what had been read was made by the parents and transcribed by the children. They also had night watches, when a few would stay up between 9.0 and 1.0 a.m., saying the psalms. The newly restored church was used regularly for services, the local parson officiating. Holy Communion would be celebrated once a month.

The work that took place every day was varied, creative, and stimulating. One major concern was to give help to the neighbouring villages. Very quickly a little school was set up in the pigeon house, and local children came there to join the children already in the community. A herb and physic garden was planted, and put to use to help cure sickness in the neighbourhood. Nicholas encouraged the children of the district to learn psalms by heart. As soon as a child could say one to him they would be rewarded with a penny and then were given their dinner as well, Nicholas believing that money and meat were 'strong allurements'. They gave 'water grewell' to the poor of the neighbourhood three times a week. They kept cows in the summer, and the poor had the milk. They rented out land around them ('lordships') to various tradesmen such as butchers and bakers, and these provided the community with food. They erected an almshouse for four poor widows in one part of the house and these old ladies became part of the family.

But these were only a small part of their activities .Much music was made: there was an organ in the great room, and they met there to sing together. Embroidery was one of the crafts they practised, and another, which absorbed more of their time and interest, was the printing of books. Nicholas asked a bookbinder's daughter from Cambridge to come and teach them the craft. They devised their own method of printing: one of the books they made was a concordance of the four evangelists, and the way they did it was to cut out certain verses with their 'Cizars' and paste them on sheets of paper, and then print from them on presses. It took them a year .They had a special room, which they called the Concordance room; it was painted green and had texts all round the walls. King Charles I heard of this concordance, and commissioned them to make one for him of the books of Kings and Chronicles. This took them another year. They presented it to him magnificently bound 'in purple velvet and richly gilt', and when he saw it he said it was 'one of the best he ever saw of its kind, which did character the Master of it, to be a man of rare parts every way'.

This remarkable commune thrived in harmonious peace and happiness under Nicholas Ferrar's guidance until his death in 1637, and was able to go on without him until 1646, when parliamentary troops despoiled the house and the church, and the community was broken up and dispersed. During all the years there, until George Herbert's death in 1633, he and Ferrar were writing to one another, and becoming closer and closer in understanding and sympathy. Their letters to each other often began 'My Exceeding Deare Brother' and are filled with affectionate respect. Had Herbert lived longer, he might have moved to live nearer to Little Gidding.

Dr.Muriel Bradbrook, in her 'T.S.Eliot' (from the series 'Writers and their Work', first published by Longman's in 1950) describes Little Gidding thus:

'It was to be known and loved by George Herbert...and to remain as perhaps the most perfect example of that exquisite blend of piety, learning, decency, and comeliness of life which distinguished the religious life of the seventeenth century at its best.'

The Ferrar family finally settled in Little Gidding in May 1626. On July 5th of that same year Herbert became the prebendary of a parish less than four miles from Little Gidding: Leighton Bromsgrove. That certainly could not have been a mere coincidence. Nicholas wanted him to come and live near them all, and it must have been because of him that Herbert selected that parish . He never in fact lived there, but Nicholas's brother John records how much he wanted to:

'Mr Herbert seeing, he could not draw Gidding nearer him, he would draw nearer to his brother N.F. and not long before his death, was upon exchanging his Living for one.....as being near his dear Brother, tho' in valew much inferior to his owne; but he sayd, that he valewed Mr. F.'s near neighbourhood more than any living. And truly there was no loss of affection between them, N.F. prizing him as a most pretious friend, and with whom he could live and dye, if God saw it good for both.'

Sadly God did not see it good for them to live near each other: Herbert died before he was able to change his parish. But nevertheless he and Ferrar did both become closely involved with the church at Leighton. John Ferrar again:

> ...'seing the fair Church of Layton was fallen down a long time.....N.F. very earnestly hereupon assaults his Brother Herbert, to sett to the work, and to try, what he could do among his friends, towards so good a work: N.F. promising all the assistance he could in that kind...'.

Herbert agreed to do all he could to restore the church. He solicited his family and friends for funds, and provided some of his own money, and Nicholas Ferrar put his brother John in charge of the work, 'by three times a week attending the workmen, and providing all materials'. Eventually, John reported, 'a fine neat church was erected, Inside and out finished.....to the admiration of all men, how such a structure should be raysed, and brought to pass by Mr. Herbert.'The work was not completed in Herbert's lifetime, as the major work of restoration, after enough money had been collected, did not begin until the summer of 1632.But the church of St. Mary at Leighton Bromsgrove still exists today in beauty and dignity, thanks to the combined inspiration of Nicholas Ferrar, his brother John, and George Herbert.

This was not their only co-operative creation. Both Ferrar and Herbert were translators, and sent each other their respective efforts. Ferrar sent Herbert his translations of the works of Valdesso, Lessus and Carbo, and Herbert wrote an introduction to the Valdesso. Herbert sent Ferrar his translation of Cornarus's Treatise on Temperance and Sobriety. And eventually, from his death bed, Herbert sent Ferrar his collected poems in English, The Temple. John Ferrar described his brother's reaction to these poems:

'And when Mr. Herbert dy'd, he recommended only of all his Papers that of his Divine Poems, and willed it to be delivered into the hands of his brother N.F. appointing him to be the Midwife, to bring that piece into the World, If he so thought good of it, else to burn it. The which when N.F. had many and many a time read over, and embraced and kissed again and again, he sayd, he could not sufficiently admire it, as a rich Jewell, and most worthy to be in the hands and hearts of all true Christians, that feared God, and loved the Church of England.'

Ferrar then set about having the poems transcribed by his nieces Anna and Mary Collett at Little Gidding, so that he could send them to the Vice-Chancellor of Cambridge to be licensed for publication. Thomas Buck, the University printer, was known to be one of the finest printers of his day, which is probably why Ferrar chose to have them printed in Cambridge rather than London. The transcribing was a long and laborious process, but even so, the work had been published by October 1633, only seven months after Herbert's death in March. Ferrar himself wrote the introduction. It can be found in the Appendix, in the original spelling, at the end of this book. Without his dedicated work, the world might never have known this marvellous collection of poems.

Nicholas Ferrar died in 1637: he was only forty six. A few months before he died he wrote a strange prediction of what he thought death would mean. It is as relevant to all of us now as then. It is revealing, because so unexpected.

'The remembrance of death is very powerful to restrain us from sinning. For he who shall well consider that the day will come(and he knoweth not how soon) when he shall be laid on a sick bed, weak and faint, without ease and almost without strength, encompassed with melancholy thoughts, and overwhelmed with anguish; when, on one side, his distemper increasing upon him, the physician tells him that he is past all hope of life, and on the other, his friends urge him to dispose of all his worldly goods and share his wealth among them: that wealth which he procured with trouble, and preserved with anxiety: that wealth which he

now parts from with sorrow: when again the Priest calls
on him to take the preparatory measures for his departure:
when he himself now begins to be assured that here he hath
no abiding city;that this is no more a world for him:that no
more Suns will rise and set upon him:that for him there will
be no more seeing, no more hearing, no more speaking, no
more touching, no more tasting, no more fancying, no more
understanding, no more remembering, no more desiring,
no more loving, no more delights of any sort to be enjoyed
by him, but that death will at one stroke deprive him of all
these things: that he will speedily be carried out of the house
which he called his own, and is now become another's:that
he will be put into a cold, narrow grave: that earth will be
consigned to earth, ashes to ashes, and dust to dust:let any
man duly and daily ponder these things, and how can it be
that he should dare......'

He stopped writing there, not having finished the thought which
inspired the whole outpouring. That he should dare...? to forget, for an
instant, what his fate is to be? to forget that a final judgment is awaiting
him? to take his life for granted? to pretend that he is immortal? The
whole subject seems to have overwhelmed him, and he can be imagined
laying down his pen at that point with a gesture of despair.

Just before he died, he asked that all his books, which he had kept
carefully ever since he came to Little Gidding, and which consisted of
light hearted reading: 'comedies, tragedies, love hymns, heroical poems,
and such like' should be burnt. " 'Carry', said he, 'those hampers to
the place of my grave, and upon it see that you burn them all' ". (John
Ferrar.) Blackstone comments: 'Only on his death-bed can Nicholas
bring himself to destroy the memorials of that life which he had long
ago deserted for ever.'

But on his death bed, he had a sudden revelation. John Ferrar describes
the scene. After Nicholas had been asked how he did, he answered:

'Pretty well, I thank my God, and you and I shall be better:'
and then he lay very still above half an houre, and more, all
standing by him, supposing him to be in a fine slumber.

But afterwards, he on a sodayn casting his hands out of the bed, with great strength, and looking up, and about with a strong voice, and cheerfull, sayd, "Oh, what a blessed change is here, what do I see? O let us come, and sing prayses to the Lord, and magnify his Holy name together. I have been at a great Feast, O magnify the Lord with me." One of his nieces sayd presently,"at a great feast, dear Father?" "I", (replyed he), "at a great feast, The Great King's Feast."

These were his last words. It is impossible not to link them with Herbert's last poem, Love II, ' Love Bade Me Welcome', when Herbert thinks of himself at a feast given by his Lord, whom he calls Love. Ferrar must have known that poem so well that it was a part of him, and it is inspiring to think of Herbert's finest poem being in his mind as he died, giving him that final great surge of certainty and strength.

T.S.Eliot helped to immortalise the community of Little Gidding in the last of his Four Quartets. He only spent one day there, visiting the chapel, in May 1936, and wrote the poem five years later while living in London during the Blitz, when it seemed as if the war might be lost, and a sense of depression fills the poem.

> Who then devised the torment? Love.
> Love is the unfamiliar Name
> Behind the hands that wove
> The intolerable shirt of flame
> Which human power cannot remove.
> We only live, only suspire
> Consumed by either fire or fire.

> With the voice of this Love and the voice of this Calling

> We shall not cease from exploration
> And the end of all our exploring
> Will be to arrive where we started
> And know the place for the first time.

But he ends the poem with Julian of Norwich's optimism:

> And all shall be well
> And all manner of thing shall be well
> When the tongues of flame are in-folded
> Into the crowned knot of fire
> and the fire and the rose are one.

Nicholas Ferrar with his asceticism, his faith and his example of true Christianity, was a source of inspiration to a great poet three centuries after his death, and will continue to be an inspiration to all those who know about him.

Chapter Four
TIME OF DECISION

George Herbert held the post of orator to Cambridge University until 1628, but he was no longer living in Cambridge after 1625. His stint at Westminster as member of parliament for the borough of Montgomery had been brief - probably only during the months of February to May 1624 - and there is no record of him actually attending during the first parliament in Charles I's reign in 1625, although his name is included in the printed list of members. Parliament was prorogued after the first session of the 1623/1624 parliament, which ended in May 1624, so there was no second session, and by the end of 1625 another man held the seat of Montgomery borough. But those few weeks in parliament were apparently enough to allow him to realise that his ambitions for his future life did not lie in the direction of politics.

Izaak Walton, who wrote his biography of George Herbert forty years after Herbert's death, was not therefore totally reliable. He did not know, for instance, that Herbert was a member of parliament. His account of Herbert's life is panegyric, to say the least, and should not be taken as gospel truth. One thing he famously wrote of was Herbert's 'court hopes'. His position as Orator was a good jumping-off ground for promotion to a position at court. Two of his predecessors in the position had gone on to high offices. Herbert was (according to Walton) 'very high in the king's favour, and not meanly loved by the most eminent and most powerful of the court nobility', and, also according to Walton, the king gave him the sinecure of the rectory of Whitford - the same as Queen Elizabeth gave to her favourite Sir Philip Sidney- worth £120 per annum. Walton says, 'with this, he enjoyed his genteel humour for clothes and court-like company.' He tells us Herbert often thought of leaving Cambridge and studying - both were bad for his health: he was inclined to consumption and fevers. He says, 'he had too thoughtful a wit; a wit like a pen knife in too narrow a sheath, too sharp for his body.' But his mother, Walton says, would not allow him to leave Cambridge, and she wanted him to take holy orders. He had to make the hard decision between that and 'the painted pleasures of court life.' During his time as orator Herbert had had much dealing with King James and his courtiers; he had influential brothers - his brother Edward was at one time ambassador to France, and his brother Henry had a court appointment as Master of the King's Revels. The Earl of Pembroke, a close and loyal supporter of the king, was a kinsman. His mother Magdalene knew all the prominent people of the day. Had Herbert wanted it enough he could most probably have joined the court in some capacity. According to Walton, his court-hopes died when some of his powerful friends there died: the Duke of Lennox; the Duke of Richmond, and the Marquis of Hamilton. But Herbert decided to be ordained deacon in 1624, just before the death of his other powerful patron, the king himself, who did not die until 1625. Becoming a deacon insured that he would eventually become an ordained priest, and no longer eligible for high court appointments.

Again according to Walton, his friends at court attempted to dissuade him, saying it was too mean an employment, and below his birth, and Walton tells us that Herbert's reply to a 'Court friend' was:

> 'It hath been formerly judged that the domestic servants of the King of Heaven should be of the noblest families on earth. And though the iniquity of the late times have made clergymen meanly valued, and the sacred name of the priest contemptible; yet I will labour to make it honourable, by consecrating all my learning, and all my poor abilities to advance the glory of that God that gave them; knowing that I can never do too much for him, that hath done so much for me as to make me a Christian.'

Walton does not say exactly where this quotation comes from, but it certainly has the genuine ring of Herbert's voice.

Eventually his decision was made. During the six months leave he was granted from the oratorship in 1624, he took the irrevocable step of being ordained deacon in the Church of England. Through his friend John Williams, who had been at St. John's College Cambridge when Herbert was at Trinity, and who had by 1624 become Dean of Westminster and Bishop of Lincoln, he was able to be ordained deacon without waiting the statutory year expected after first declaring his intention to join the church. The ceremony took place before the end of 1624. To be a deacon in the church of England is a lesser position than that of priest: he cannot celebrate communion or give absolution, but he has committed himself to having taken holy orders. Williams also arranged for Herbert to become a 'comportioner' (part-holder) of the rectory of Llandinam, Montgomeryshire - only a short distance from where he was born. This happened on 6th December 1624. Herbert held this preferment until he died, and gained a small income from it, but he never lived there. Although he was now fully committed to a life in holy orders, he did not become a fully fledged priest until 1630.

From 1625 until 1629 Herbert's life is largely unchronicled. Walton tells us that just after James I died in 1625 Herbert 'betook himself to a retreat from London, to a friend in Kent, where he lived very privately, and was such a lover of solitariness, as was judged to impair his health, more than his study had done.' It is known also that in 1625 he was occupied with his family. His older sister Margaret Vaughan had died in 1623, leaving three young daughters, Dorothy, Margaret and Katherine, and their father was already dead. George as the oldest of the younger surviving uncles - his older surviving brothers Edward and Henry both being abroad at the time - was the one left to take responsibility, with his mother, for the children. None of them in 1623 can have been older than sixteen, as Margaret was married in 1606. His mother and Edward became their co-guardians, but George felt a particular duty towards them, and much later took them to live with him.

During 1625, the year of a great plague in London, Herbert was also staying with his mother and stepfather in Chelsea. This we know from John Donne, who in order to escape the plague went to stay with the Danvers, and noted laconically in a letter, 'Mr. George Herbert is here.' Amy M. Charles speculates in her biography of Herbert, on the relationship between the two men:

> 'Trying to imagine how these two witty, devout men met and talked can furnish us with the best of imaginary conversations.

Two brilliant and resourceful poets, neither likely to give
himself easily, both capable of exciting great admiration
in their hearers, both accomplished speakers, quick, alert,
mercurial - what sort of conversations *did* they have in the
handsome house and the stately Italian gardens?'

It is certain that Donne's influence on Herbert, his junior by
nineteen years, was profoundly important. Herbert had taken the first
step towards becoming a priest, but that did not mean, as his poetry
shows, that it was an easy decision. In 1625 Donne was Dean of St.Paul's
Cathedral in London - a position given to him by King James in 1621
- but he himself had had years of indecision before he joined the church
in 1614. He too had possibly hoped for more worldly success at court,
and had found losing that privileged existence hard to contemplate .
So he knew the conflicts Herbert had wrestled with, and he knew
how such a rich, brilliant mind could fear that constrictions might be
possible in the narrower life that had been chosen. But both men were
able - and no doubt they helped each other - to rise above what might
to lesser men have been the narrowness of their vocation, and make
it something rich, rare and wonderful, and of infinite inspiration to
succeeding generations.

The next step on the ecclesiastical ladder was Herbert's appointment,
also through John Williams, as canon of Lincoln Cathedral, and at
the same time, as prebendary of Leighton Bromswold, beside Little
Gidding, and not far from Lincoln. These two appointments took
place on 6th July 1626, and both were by proxy. He was not there
himself because as orator he was involved in making the oration at the
ceremony installing the Duke of Buckingham as the new chancellor
of Cambridge University, on July 14th. Apart from this oration it seems
that after Herbert left Cambridge in 1624 the duties of orator were
largely taken over by the deputy orator, Herbert Thorndyke, and later
by Robert Creighton who succeeded Herbert as orator in 1628.

In 1626 Herbert suffered from what Walton called 'a sharp quotidian
ague', and went to stay with his brother Henry in Woodford, Essex. He
managed to cure himself, up to a point, by his diet: 'forbearing Drink,
and not eating any Meat, no not Mutton, nor a Hen, or Pigeon, unless
they were salted: and by such a constant diet, he removed his Ague.'

He probably stayed in Essex until his mother became so ill, in 1627, that he had to go back to be with her in Chelsea. She died in early June 1627, in her early sixties. Walton tells us of her funeral, at which he was present, and John Donne preached: 'I saw and heard this Mr. John Donne - who was then Dean of St. Paul's - weep, and preach her Funeral Sermon, in the Parish Church of Chelsea, near London.'

It is moving to read this lengthy and brilliant sermon remembering that every word, as it was delivered, was heard by her devoted son George, grieving in the congregation. It adds poignancy to Donne's affectionate description of a woman he had greatly admired ever since he first met her in Oxford twenty seven years before. He described her second marriage, to the much younger Sir John Danvers, in this way :

> '.....her personall, and naturall endowments, had their part in drawing, and fixing the affections of such a person, as by his birth, and youth, and interest in great favours in Court, and legal proximity to great possessions in the world, might justly have promist him acceptance, in what family soever, hee had directed, and plac't his affections. He plac't them here; neither diverted them, nor repented since. For, as the well tuning of an Instrument, makes higher and lower strings, of one sound, so the inequality of their yeeres, was thus reduc't to an evennesse, that shee had a cheerfulnesse, agreeable to his youth, and he a sober staidness, conformable to her more yeeres.'

Donne goes on with a lengthy description of her qualities:

> '...to this consideration of her person then, belongs this, that God gave her such a comelinesse, as, though she were not proud of it, yet she was so content with it, as not to goe about to mend it, by any art.

> '... shee never diverted towards the Papist, in undervaluing the Scriptures, nor towards the Separatist, in undervaluing the Church..... but in the doctrine and discipline of that Church... she brought up her children.

In its entirety the sermon is a wonderfully comprehensive assessment of a remarkable woman.

There is no doubt of the strong bond between her and George, who was probably her favourite son. At the time of her death he wrote the Memoriae Matris Sacrum, also known as the Parentalia, and this long work, consisting of nineteen poems, fourteen in Latin and five in Greek, must have been his main preoccupation in the sad days after her death, as the whole work was finished in time for it to be printed with Donne's sermon in the Stationers' Register, on July 7th. George had been her devoted and obedient son all his life, but after her death it is significant that he felt able at last to resign from the oratorship: something she had not encouraged him to do. And shortly after her death he came into a small inheritance from the sale of a property - the manor of Ribblesford in Gloucestershire - and so was able to have a larger measure of financial independence as well. He had no commitments, apart from that of canon of Lincoln Cathedral, and of Leighton Ecclesia, and these did not entail much work, apart from his own desire to rebuild the Leighton church, and to persuade people to subscribe to its rebuilding. It was soon after his mother's death that he decided to go and live in Wiltshire, and he stayed in that county for the rest of his life.

The house he chose to go to was that of his stepfather's older brother, the Earl of Danby, who lived at Dauntesey, near Chippenham. He moved there in 1628, and that same year his stepfather married again, to Elizabeth Dauntesey, and through her became co-owner of the estate of Lavington in Wiltshire, where he again set about creating a fine garden. Herbert was in constant touch with his stepfather, and eventually made him the overseer of his will. And he was to find the woman whom he married in 1629 in his stepfather's family.

Moving to Wiltshire was the beginning, for George Herbert, of the final and most rewarding years of his life. The death of his mother must have been for him a hollow desolation, but it was also a liberation. She had provided him with so much love, attention and guidance that there was hardly room in his life for another woman. But in 1628 he was thirty five years old, and knew that he needed a wife. Either through his stepfather or his brother Lord Danby he had met the daughter of their kinsman Mr. Charles Danvers, of Baynton House, in the parish of Edington, about twenty miles south of Dauntesey, on the edge of

Salisbury plain. Mr. Charles Danvers had nine daughters. He had died by the time Herbert came to live in Wiltshire, but according to Walton, he had persuaded his daughter Jane that George Herbert was the man she should marry, and had also told George that Jane was the woman for him. Walton tells us that the moment they met they fell in love, and were married three days later. But Amy M. Charles finds this idea absurd: Herbert had been so closely involved with the Danvers family, since the age of sixteen when Sir John became his stepfather, that it is most unlikely that he did not know this branch of the family as well, and such a precipitate courtship and marriage was totally out of character in a man whom we know deliberated long and painfully before taking each new step in his life.

At this stage in his account of Herbert's life, Walton tells us what he looked like. He says of him:

> 'He was of a stature inclined to tallness, his body was very straight, and so far from being cumbered with too much flesh, that he was lean to an extremity. His aspect was cheerful, and his speech and motion did both declare him a gentleman.'

In contrast, John Aubrey in his 'Brief Lives' describes Jane, who was his cousin, as 'a handsome bona roba and ingeniose.' Bona roba meant that she had a full well-rounded body, and ingeniose meant that she was an intelligent person. So these two contrastingly-shaped people came together to be married, in the parish church of Edington, on 5th March, 1629. Herbert then moved from Dauntesey and lived with his new wife, her brothers and sisters, and her widowed mother, at Baynton House near Edington, less than twenty miles north of Wilton, the home of Herbert's kinsman the Earl of Pembroke. He lived there for more than a year, while the next step of his life was being decided.

By 1629 Herbert had been a deacon for more than four years, and he still had to decide whether he wanted to become a fully-fledged priest. In June 1629, according to Walton, the living of Fuggleston-with-Bemerton fell vacant, when the incumbent, Dr. Curle, was made Bishop of Bath and Wells. This parish lies between Wilton and Salisbury; about three miles from Wilton and less than two miles from Salisbury, and extends from the grounds of Wilton House to the west to the parish of Fisherton Anger on the east. The presentation of the living was the responsibility of King Charles, rather than the patron of the parish who was the Earl of Pembroke, as it was the king who had elevated Curle to his bishopric. But it was Lord Pembroke who urged the king to give the living to his kinsman George Herbert. Now was the time for Herbert finally to make up his mind whether he really wanted to become a humble parson of a small parish, with a rectory and church both badly in need of repair, a small stipend, and all last chances of glory on the world stage gone for ever. Walton tells us that before he made his decision he 'did fast and pray often and consider, for not less than a month.' But eventually he found, whatever his doubts and difficulties, that he was drawn irresistibly to a life of service to God. His poem 'The Collar' expresses the remorselessness of the magnet impelling him towards the priesthood, in spite of all resistance and unwillingness on his part. The last lines of the poem encapsulate his surrender:

> But as I rav'd and grew more fierce and wilde
> At every word,
> Me thoughts I heard one calling, *Child!*
> And I reply'd, *My Lord.*

The subjugation was inevitable. Herbert was far too complex a man to make such a decision easily, but his uncertainties only show how powerful was the force that eventually drew him, and drew him willingly, into his years of service as a priest of God.

The decision was made, and the induction took place on 26th April 1630. The Institution took place in Salisbury cathedral, and the induction later the same day, in his own parish church, St. Andrews, Bemerton. Walton's source for the story of the induction was Arthur Woodnoth, a cousin of Nicholas Ferrar's, who was with Herbert on April 26th, waiting outside the church, where Herbert was shut in alone, to toll the bell and to pray. After quite a long time Woodnoth looked into the church through a window, and saw Herbert lying full length on the floor, in front of the altar, deep in prayer.

The final ordination, by Bishop Davenant, took place in Salisbury cathedral on September 9th, 1630. His duties at Lincoln cathedral and Leighton Bromswold at Whitsun of that year could well have been the reason for the long delay before the final ordination. Amy M.Charles speculates that he might have travelled to Lincoln to preach in the cathedral on Whitsunday, and visited Nicholas Ferrar on the way, to persuade him to take over the prebendship of Leighton Bromsgrove. He knew he would be too far away, living near Salisbury, to do the long journey to Huntingdon and Lincoln. Ferrar agreed to take it on. This did not mean that Herbert gave up his project of raising money to restore the church at Leighton Bromsgrove: he successfully raised enough, through his family and rich friends, for the work to be completed soon after his death.

And that was not his only rebuilding work. The rectory and church and small chapel at Bemerton all needed restoration. The church was tackled first, then the chapel and the rectory, and he and his wife were able to move in to the first home of his own he had ever had, before the end of 1630. Walton tells us he had some lines of verse 'writ upon, or engraven, in the mantle of the Chimney in his Hall' of the rectory.

To My Successor.

'If thou chance for to find
A new House to thy mind
And built without thy Cost
Be good to the Poor,
As God gives thee store,
And then, my Labour's not lost.

Sadly, when the rectory was restored in the nineteenth century there was no sign of the inscription when the plaster was taken off round the 'massive chimney mantel'. But the inscription (without its title) has been carved roughly on a stone tablet and set in to the outside wall above the front door of the rectory, facing the church. It does not look like the lettering Herbert would have used, and must have been done some time after he died. And this inscrition has now been granted a new immortality. The present Archbishop of Canterbury, Rowan Williams, for his enthronement ceremony in Canterbury cathedral on 26th February 2003 (which is known as the Feast of George Herbert, Priest and Poet, in the Church of England calendar) commissioned a fine anthem by the composer James MacMillan, using the words of the inscription. Two of Herbert's poems were sung as hymns during the service, and the archbishop quoted the final words of 'Love:III' in his sermon, ending the sermon with these words:

> "And he (Christ) says to us.......'Learn from them (the child, the poor, the forgotten), and you will find a life's work; and you will find rest for your souls; you will come home, *you will sit and eat.*'"

Herbert has thus been set in the centre of the sensibility of the Church of England at the beginning of the 21st century - 370 years after his death.

Herbert had used £200 of his own money in the restoration of the rectory. After he died, the house became the home for all future rectors of Bemerton, until the late 20th century, when it was sold by the Ecclesiatical authorities. Since then it has had four secular owners, of whom Vikram Seth, the writer, is the fourth and present owner.

Although the front of the house lies directly on a busy road which divides it from the little church, no noise of traffic can be heard in the rooms which face the other way, across the garden. There is a feeling of peace in all these rooms. Nearly every room is filled with books, and tranquil, contemplative calm pervades the house, as it must have in Herbert's day. The windows face out on to a long lawn which slopes down to the little river - the Nadder. There are acres of wild woodland belonging to the house, with deer wandering through them, and the river is well stocked with fish. It is easy to imagine Jane Herbert overseeing the management of her garden and her farm animals in the little estate.

The room in which George Herbert is thought to have died had, in his day, a stone window facing across the road to the church, and another bigger window facing across the lawn to the river, and, away to the left, to the spire of Salisbury cathedral. Standing in that room it is impossible not to feel a weight of sadness that such a man had to die there before he had reached his fortieth birthday.We do know that before he died he had attained the peace of mind and sense of fufillment that he had sought through his life, but had he lived longer, what further glories might he have created?

Izaak Walton, in his eulogistic biography, continues his account of Herbert's life:

'I have now brought him to the Parsonage of Bemerton, and to the thirty-sixth year of his age, and must stop here, and bespeak the Reader to prepare for an almost incredible story, of the great sanctity of the short remainder of his holy life; a life so full of charity, humility, and all Christian virtues, that it deserves the eloquence of St. Chrysostom to commend and declare it: a life, that if it were related by a pen like his, there would then be no need for this age to look back into times past for the examples of primitive piety; for they might all be found in the life of George Herbert.'

On the next page he gives Herbert's conversation with Arthur Woodnoth - which he assures us was as Woodnoth himself reported it. Woodnoth was indeed known to Walton, but had died thirty years before he wrote this account, so there may be some licence of interpretation in the words he gives us. He tells us that on the same night of the induction Herbert said to Woodnoth:

'I now look back upon my aspiring thoughts, and think myself more happy than if I had attained what I then so ambitiously thirsted for. And now I can behold the Court with an impartial eye, and see plainly that it is made up of fraud and titles, and flattery, and many other such empty, imaginary, painted pleasures, that are so empty, as not to satisfy when they are enjoyed. But in God, and his service, is a fulness of all joy and pleasure, and no satiety.'

Walton's life is worth reading, not necessarily for its accuracy, but for the picture he left posterity of a man of whom, had it not been for this Life, we would know little - and the picture is so charitable and so delightful that we can only be grateful for it, even if we cannot wholly rely on it. Amy M. Charles's 'A Life of George Herbert' published in 1977 gives a far more accurately reliable picture and often gently corrects Walton's assumptions.

George Herbert was ready, at last, to give his whole life to the service of God.

Chapter Five

THE LAST YEARS AT BEMERTON

After George and Jane Herbert moved into Bemerton rectory they had less than three years left to live together before George's death in 1633. So much had to be achieved in that short time. When they moved there George's health had seemed to be good, but he had been battling against consumption since his stay with his brother Henry in Woodford, and taking on, most conscientiously, the commitments of a country parson, must have placed great strain on his strength.

One of the first things he did after they got there was to bring the three orphaned daughters of his sister Margaret to live with them. One of his few existing letters is the one he wrote to his brother Henry, in the autumn of 1630, about the three nieces. Their older brother Edward had written to George suggesting that he should have *one* of the nieces to live with them. Herbert explained to Henry:

'I wrote to (Edward) that I would have both or neither; and that upon this ground, that they were to come into an unknown country, tender in knowledge, sense, and age, and knew none but one who could be no company to them. Therefore I considered that if only one came, the comfort intended would be a discomfort. Since that I have seen the fruit of my observation, for they have lived so lovingly, lying, eating, walking, praying, working still together, that I take a comfort therein; and would not have to part them yet........ It is true there is a third sister, whom to receive were the greatest charitie of all, for she is youngest, and least looked unto; having none to doe it but her school-mistresse, and you know what those mercenary creatures are. Neither hath she any to repair unto at good times, as Christmas, etc.........If you could think of taking her, as once you did, surely it were a great good deed, ...yet, truly if you take her not, I am thinking to do it, even beyond my strengthe; especially at this time, being more beggarly now than I have been these many yeares, as having spent two hundred pounds in building; which to me that have nothing yett, is very much.'

Indeed, Herbert did have all three sisters to live with him at Bemerton. The oldest, Margaret, died shortly before he did, in 1632. If only there were more of his letters! This one shows such sensitivity, combined with worldly good sense, as he worries about the little girl being left at Christmas-time to the devices of a mercenary schoolmistress.

The rectory was not a large house, but Amy M. Charles reports that besides himself, his wife and three nieces, they had four maidservants and two manservants living with them. It faced south, and the spire of Salisbury cathedral could be seen from the bottom of the garden, where the river Nadder runs. The walk to the cathedral was along a footpath on the bank of the river.

We know from Walton, that Herbert sang twice every week in Salisbury.

'His chiefest recreation was Music, in which heavenly art he was a most excellent master, and did himself compose many Divine Hymns and Anthems, which he set and sang to his lute or viol: and though he was a lover of retiredness, yet his love of Music was such, that he went usually twice every week, on certain appointed days, to the Cathedral Church in Salisbury; and at his return would say 'that his time spent in prayer, and Cathedral-music elevated his soul, and was his Heaven upon earth.' But before his return thence to Bemerton, he would usually sing and play his part at an appointed private Music-meeting.

The composers whose music he must have sung and played would have been the English composers Tallis, Taverner, William Byrd, Christopher Tye, Thomas Morley, John Bull, Thomas Campion, John

Weelkes, Philip Rosseter. He must have known and loved the madrigals of Thomas Tomkins, the brother of the choirmaster at Salisbury; and he must also have known the music of Palestrina and Monteverdi, Orlando Lassus and Tomas Victoria. It is strange to think that he could not possibly have known the music of Henry Purcell, who was not born until 1658, or of Johann Sebastian Bach and Georg Friedrich Handel, both born in 1685. I'm sure he must have loved to sing the masses and madrigals of William Byrd, whom he had known as a child when Byrd visited his mother's house in Charing Cross. Perhaps, by 1630, his group were contemporary enough to know the music of the German composer Heinrich Schutz, who bridged the gap between the early contrapuntal music of Palestrina and Byrd, and the later contrapuntal music of Bach and Handel. Schutz was born eight years earlier than Herbert, and would have seemed modern and challenging.

The tutor of the choristers at Salisbury when Herbert came to Bemerton was Gyles Tomkins, one of several musical brothers who held posts as organist in other cathedrals, the most famous being Thomas Tomkins who was for fifty years the organist of Worcester cathedral. When Gyles Tomkins was appointed to this post, in 1629, his last position had been as organist at King's College Cambridge, and so it is extremely likely that he and Herbert knew each other, as Herbert had only left Cambridge five years earlier. When Tomkins arrived at Salisbury he was indirectly the cause of a tremendous rumpus. The previous tutor of the choristers, John Holmes, had died, and his widow, wanting to see her son-in-law John Clark succeed him, refused to move out of the chorister's house to allow Tomkins to move in. Deadlock was reached, and the furore came to the august ears of the Archbishop of Canterbury, and the royal ears of Charles I. Tomkins was not able to move into the chorister's house until December 1630. The choir suffered from all this tension: in fact it was more or less disbanded in October 1629. But by 1634, when Archbishop Laud visited Salisbury, it was restored, and Gyles Tomkins given the credit for their good singing. Herbert must have approved of the standard of singing, to go so regularly to hear Evensong in the cathedral.

The choir consisted of six vicars chorall, in holy orders; seven singing men, one of which was teacher of the choristers and one the organist, and six boy choristers. At Herbert's funeral in 1633 the singing men and choristers sang the burial office in the little Bemerton church. Amy M.Charles speculates that in the music-making in the cathedral close Herbert may well have sung some of his own poems to his own music, accompanying himself on the lute. If so, his singing companions would have been among the first people to realise that the rector of Bemerton was a remarkable writer of poetry.

Along with his parochial duties, about which he was most conscientious, Herbert found time to write. Apart from poems, which he was writing privately for himself all the time, he wrote a prose work which he meant to be read by other men aspiring to be country parsons as he was, and also, as he said in his preface, for himself.

> 'I have resolved to set down the Form and Character of a True Pastour, that I may have a Mark to aim at: which also I will set as high as I can, since hee shoots higher that threatens the Moon, than hee that aims at a Tree.'

(His typically satirical, humorous voice proclaims itself in the words 'threatens the Moon'.)

This was a work of thirty seven chapters, each one giving guidance on some aspect of a parson's duties to his parishioners. For instance, ChapterVIII is called 'The Parson on Sundays'; Chapter XII 'The Parson's Charity'; Chapter XV 'The Parson Comforting'; Chapter XXIV, 'The Parson Arguing'. Such a document had never before - or since - been written . It was not published in Herbert's lifetime. He finished it in 1632, according to the Preface. It is now known as 'The Country Parson', although the title given it when first published by Barnabus Oley in 1652 was more cumbersome: 'A Priest to the Temple, or, The Country Parson, His Character, Etc.' Barnabus Oley was given it by the Reverend Edmond Duncon, rector of Fryarn-Barnet, who was with Herbert as he was dying. Arthur Woodnot, who was also at Herbert's deathbed, may first have had the manuscript, and have given it to Duncon later - but the man who eventually published it said Duncon gave it to him.

The various chapters are delightful to read, and give us a vibrant picture of Herbert's own character. It is clear from them that he had no illusions about his parishioners: he saw them exactly for what they were. In Chapter VI, 'The Parson Praying' he gives a graphic description of how a congregation might behave:

'He having often instructed his people how to carry themselves in the divine service, exacts of them all possible reverence, by no means enduring either talking, or sleeping, or gazing, or leaning, or half-kneeling, or any other undutifull behaviour in them....'

When they are giving the responses, he tells them:

'which answers also are to be done not in a hudling, or slubbering fashion, gaping, or scratching the head, or spitting even in the midst of their answer, but gently and pausably, thinking what they say.'

The poor of the parish are not the only ones he watches caustically:

'If there be any of the gentry or nobility of the Parish, who sometimes make it a piece of state not to come at the beginning of service with their poor neighbours, but at mid-prayers, both to their own loss, and of theirs also who gaze upon them when they come in, and neglect the present service of God, he by no means suffers it, but after divers gentle admonitions, if they persevere, he causes them to be presented: or if the poor Church-wardens be affrighted with their greatness, notwithstanding his instruction that they ought not to be so, but even to let the world sinke, so they do their duty; he presents them himself, only protesting to them that not any ill will draws him to it, but the debt and obligation of his calling, being to obey God rather than men.'

In Chapter VIII, 'The Parson on Sundays', he shows his practical down-to-earth attitude to his calling:

'The Country Parson, as soon as he awakes on Sunday morning, presently falls to work, and seems to himself so as a Market-man is, when the Market day comes, or a shopkeeper, when customers come in. His thoughts are full of making the best of the day, and contriving it to his best gaines.'

He gives good advice to unmarried parsons in Chapter IX, 'The Parson's state of Life':

If he be unmarryed, and sojourne, he never talkes with any woman alone, but in the audience of others, and that seldom, and then also in a serious manner, never jestingly or sportfully.'

Another cogent sentence in this chapter is his advice not to try to be too clever:

'Curiosity in prying into high speculative and unprofitable questions, is another great stumbling block to the holiness of Scholars.'

We learn so much of Herbert himself from these perceptive little essays on the do's and dont's of a parson's life. In Chapter IV, 'The Parson preaching' he explains how to keep his congregation's attention:

'Sometimes he tells them stories, and sayings of others, according as his text invites him; for them also men heed, and remember them better than exhortations which though earnest yet often dy with the sermon, especially with country people, which are thick, and heavy, and hard to raise to the point of zeal, and fervency, and need a mountain of fire to kindle them.'

His sense of humour must often have saved him from feelings of acute frustration.

Further on in this chapter he has a lovely metaphor:

'(A Parson procures attention....) by dipping and seasoning all our words in our hearts, before they come into our mouths, truly affecting, and cordially expressing, all we say;

so that the auditors may plainly perceive that every word is hart-deep.'

'Hart-deep' is what all Herbert's writing is, which is why, as we read his poetry, our own hearts are suddenly captured and entranced. None of Herbert's sermons have survived. But 'The Country Parson' gives an illuminating hint of how fine they must have been.

Herbert found time to do much writing during his few years at Bemerton. Not only 'The Country Parson' and the revising of earlier poems and writing of new ones, but also translating Cornaro's treatise on Temperance, and annotating his friend Nicholas Ferrar's translation of Valdesso's Considerations. The first of these was published in Cambridge after Herbert's death, in 1634, together with other translations of works on health and dietary matters by Lessius and Carbone, in a small volume called Hygiasticon. Walton tells us that there were other of Herbert's writings which were destroyed by fire at the home of his widow. In 1639 she married Sir Robert Cook, and their house at Highnam near Gloucester was burnt during the Civil War.

The Rev. F.E.Hutchinson, in his Oxford Complete Works of George Herbert, published a collection of proverbs, entitled 'Outlandish Proverbs', but with some hesitation as to whether Herbert was responsible for all of them. 'Outlandish' meant they were mainly foreign, many being translated from Italian, French and Spanish. Collecting proverbs was a hobby people enjoyed during and before Herbert's lifetime. Erasmus had a collection in The Adagio; Francis Bacon compiled a collection which he called 'A Promus of Formularies and Excellencies' - and Herbert's brothers Edward and Henry both collected them, many of whose appear in Herbert's list. There are 1,184, first published together in 1640, and attributed to George, who showed a delight in them, and used them in his poems, especially in the long poem 'The Sacrifice', in which many of the verses contain a proverb. Herbert must have collected them as other people collect stamps or matchboxes: a light-hearted hobby with underlying gleams of seriousness, in the succinct wisdom so many of them hold. A letter written after Herbert's death by Nicholas Ferrar's brother John to his son makes it certain Herbert had a hand in collecting them: he tells him that when he comes into his inheritance he should devote a twentieth part of it to God, "remembering daily those two

Divine Verses of your uncle's most Deare friend of whom it was said by those that knew them both there was one soule in two bodies) -

> 'Great almes Giving lessens no mans living'
> and
> 'By giving to the Poore we Increase our Store.'"

These are number 190 and 191 in 'Outlandish Proverbs'.
Several of the collection are funny, such as
No. 203. Diseases of the eye are to be cured by the elbow.
No. 219. Into a shut mouth flies flie not.
No. 336. Since you know all, and I nothing, tell me what I dreamed last night.
No. 828. Better a snotty child, than his nose wip'd off.
Some are well known now, such as
No. 196. Whose house is of glasse, must not throw stones at another.
No. 306. All is not gold that glisters.
It is easy to imagine Herbert smiling with pleasure at each new one he translated or discovered, as he added it to his long list.
Herbert died on March 1st, 1633. (In his time the new year began on March 25th, which is why his death is sometimes reported as happening in 1632/1633.) He was far too young - not quite forty - and it was at a time when all was going well for him. He had found his true vocation, and it suited him; he had a loving wife and family; he had his poetry and his music; his kinsman's fine estate was just beside him, where he often went. But he had had to struggle against ill health ever since he first went to Cambridge, and he eventually died of consumption.
Mercifully for us, he was wise enough to entrust the manuscript of his poems to his dearest friend Nicholas Ferrar. He gave the collection (it was the one which is now known as 'B', for Bodleian, and included the earlier collection now known as 'W' for Williams, some of which he had revised, and many new ones) to the Reverend Edmund Duncon, who, according to Walton, was sent by Nicholas Ferrar to visit Herbert, when he heard how ill he was. The account of this visit was actually given to Walton by Duncon himself, forty years after Herbert's death. Herbert gave him the poems three weeks before he died.

Herbert's wife Jane, his two surviving nieces, his curate Nathaniel Bostocke, and his friend Arthuir Woodnoth were with him when he died. It is due to Woodnoth that we know the date of his death, as he wrote to Nicholas Ferrar, telling him

> 'Uppon Friday, about foure a clock it pleased God to take unto his mercy the soule of our Deere Deere brother & frend Mr Harbart whose boddy uppon Sunday was buried the more particular passages of his sicknes Death and buriall I shall give yo an accompt.'

Woodnoth forgot to date his letter, but parish registers give 3rd March as the date of the funeral, and he died the Friday before. He died in his bedchamber overlooking the River Nadder. He had written his will only four days before. He is buried in Bemerton church, in an unmarked grave near the altar.

Nicholas Ferrar, knowing his friend was near death, wrote a most poignant, heartbroken prayer asking for his life to be spared. It is long and desperate. It begins:

> O most mighty and mercifull Father, we most humbly beseech thee, if it be thy good pleasure, to continue to us that singular benefit which thou hast given us in the friendship of thy servant, our dear brother, who now lieth on the bed of sickness. Let him abide with us yet a while, for the furtherance of our faith.'

Ferrar did not know that at the time he was writing this, Herbert had already died.

At the time of his death, Herbert's poetry was unknown and he himself unknown. But thanks to the immediate diligence of Ferrar in so quickly arranging the publication of the collection, which he, not Herbert, called 'The Temple: Sacred Poems and Private Ejaculations'; by the end of 1633 the work had gone through two editions, and by 1637 there had been four editions. By the end of the seventeenth century eleven editions had been published, and thirteen editions by 1709. Then there was a pause, and the next edition was published in 1799. Nicholas

Ferrar wrote a fine preface to the first edition, which will be found at the end of this book: it is worth quoting in its entirety.

Now, more that four hundred years after his birth, the poetry of George Herbert is part of the world's heritage of literature, never to be shifted from its pre-eminence among all that is most excellent in English writing. The selection of his poems that follows is a personal choice, and it is to be hoped that the personal commentaries on the poems will help to inspire the same enthusiasm as that which inspired the commentator.

ACADEMIC SOURCES.

There have been a great many excellent academic books written about George Herbert, and this does not pretend to be adding to their number, but I have used several of them while writing it. If anyone wants to study him more intensively, the following six books will be of immense value, as they were to me.

The first I used was by Elizabeth Clarke, published in 1997 by the Oxford University Press. It is entitled 'Theory and Theology in George Herbert's Poetry', and is a comprehensive analysis of literary and religious influences on his writing. Among many other influences she lists Savonarola, and the counter-reformation writings of the French St. Francois de Sales, who lived at the end of the sixteenth century. She discusses, as one of his influences, the 'ejaculatory' style of the psalms. She examines his attitude to Juan de Valdes, the Spanish writer, whose work was translated by Herbert's friend Nicholas Ferrar with Herbert's own notes attached to the text. Her book is a remarkable work of scholarship.

A second outstanding book is 'A Reading of George Herbert' by Rosamund Tuve, published in 1952 by the University of Chicago Press. In this she considers the background knowledge and influences of Herbert's contemporaries, and the necessity to be aware of these when reading his work. She relates relevant literature, pictures, symbols, stained glass, manuscripts etc. that were currently familiar at the time he was writing, and which elucidate symbols and metaphors which would otherwise be obscure to us in his writing. It is a delightful book, using pictures and stained glass current in his day to illustrate her thesis. For instance, she has an illustration from a fifteenth century manuscript showing two pictures together on the page: one is of Christ being nailed to the cross, and one is of a man hammering nails into a lyre, already strung. From this juxtaposition come two examples of conceits that we might not understand as Herbert expected us to, without her guidance. The first is in his poem 'The Temper':

> Stretch me or contract me, thy poor debter
> This is but tuning of my breast
> To make the music better.

The second comes in the poem 'Easter':

> The Crosse taught all wood to resound his name,
> Who bore the same.
> His stretched sinews taught all strings, what key
> Is best to celebrate this most high day.

This is only one example of her remarkable research into analogies which might seem far-fetched to us but were easily recognisable to his contemporaries.

A third book I found extremely useful is Amy. M. Charles's 'A Life of George Herbert', published in 1977 by the Cornell University Press. In it she questions some of the findings of Izaak Walton, who wrote his life of George Herbert in 1673 - forty years after Herbert's death, and when Walton was an old man of eighty. He was thought of as the supreme authority on the subject for at least two centuries. She found Walton's Life 'neither accurate nor dependable' - and yet it is his depiction of Herbert that has handed down a stereotype to future generations: one which only two people since have modified. One was Joseph H. Summers, in 1954 (George Herbert, His Religion and Art), and the other was the Rev. F.E.Hutchinson, who is for me a fourth and most important researcher into Herbert's life and poetry. He was responsible for editing the Oxford edition of the works of George Herbert, in 1940.This great work is the definitive edition of Herbert's writings, and includes his The County Parson, his Outlandish Proverbs, many of his letters both in English and in Latin, and some of his Latin poems and Orations. This collection is the one recommended by most scholars of Herbert. In it Hutchinson writes his own version of Herbert's life, more accurately than Walton, and includes his own comprehensive notes to the poetry and prose: these show profound scholarship. Anyone wanting the best possible collection of Herbert's work should try to find this book. Although it was reprinted many times, up to 1970, it is now out of print, but can be bought second hand with perseverance.

A fifth study well worth reading is 'The Poetry of George Herbert' written by Helen Vendler and published by Harvard University Press in 1975. The pleasure of this book comes from the wholehearted delight she herself gains from Herbert's poetry. She says of him

> He is the Schubert of English poetry, with a new ripple in every invention. A cascade of forms flashes through The Temple like one of Schubert's brooks, delighting in turns and reversals, now modest, now glittering.

She does not agree with Coleridge or Eliot that one needs to be religious oneself in order to appreciate his poetry: she offers 'a reading of Herbert which sees as the primary object of his poems the workings of his own mind and heart, rather than the expression of certain religious beliefs.'

In her detailed examination of his poems she praises many aspects, among them his extraordinarily complete perception of his own moods; his resolute unwillingness to take the world for granted; his felicity in describing the most tenuous feelings, and his 'saintly impertinence' (a phrase from William Empson). Her detailed analysis of many of his poems is invaluable.

The sixth book I recommend is by a Canadian academic : Gene Edward Veith, Jr. It is called 'Reformation Spirituality: The Religion of George Herbert ' and is published by Lewisburg, Bucknell University Press, London and Toronto: Associated University Presses in 1985. He is a scholar whose knowledge of Calvinism helped him to explain Herbert's poetry, and also, he writes in his introduction, Herbert's poetry helps to explain Calvinism. He says of Herbert that he seems to him to be one of the greatest of all religious poets, and he explains that in writing this book his thesis throughout is 'simply that Reformation spirituality and the poetry of George Herbert mutually illumine one another.'

I have been asked whether the reason that I am adding to the many books about Herbert is because I have dug up some important new facts about him, or have a totally new approach to his poetry. Neither of those is the reason for this book What I hope to achieve by writing about him is to re-introduce him, at the start of the 21st century, to people who have only a hazy idea of his merit, and to introduce him to others who may hardly ever have heard of him. It may seem impertinent to expect people to read a book about a poet which is not written by an academic scholar. But enthusiasm is infectious, and a counteraction to cynicism. Enthusiasm for Herbert the man and the poet can carry us a long way towards re-appraising our attitude towards the fast-failing Christian church, and all it stood for in his time, in our time, and, with luck, well into the third millennium. He deserves this appreciation, few English poets more so, and I hope I can help to inspire it.

INDEX OF POEMS AND COMMENTARIES

EXPLANATION OF SPELLING
AND PRONUNCIATION

The layout of the poems and their spelling have been taken from The Works of George Herbert, edited by The Rev. F.E.Hutchinson, and published by the Oxford University Press. He says in his introduction that his text is 'nearer to what Herbert intended than what has hitherto appeared.' It is the text accepted by most scholars as the most reliable.

For the pronunciation: Herbert put in apostrophes when he did not wish the syllable to be sounded. Where there is no apostrophe the syllable should be accorded a full beat in the metre.

The poems are grouped according to their subject matter.

Group One
HOW TO FIND THE WAY TO GOD

In the first three poems the direction the poet is facing is upwards, towards God in heaven. The Starre, obviously celestial, having been invited by the poet to enter his heart, shoots upwards again, to where the Saviour is in heaven. For the Pearle - a metaphor for God's love- all must be sacrificed, and then the poet can climb unencumbered towards God. The Pulley light-heartedly compares the journey towards God as a bargaining on the pulley: the weight of restlessness combined with weariness will eventually toss him up to God. In the Elixir the poet's journey is achieved through finding God in all the humble tasks of life.

The Starre.

Bright spark, shot from a brighter place,
Where beams surround my Saviours face,
        Canst thou be anywhere
        So well as there ?

Yet, if thou wilt from thence depart,
Take a bad lodging in my heart ;
        For thou canst make a debter,
        And make it better.

First with thy fire-work burn to dust
Folly, and worse than folly, lust :
        Then with thy light refine,
        And make it thine.

So disengag'd from sinne and sicknesse
Touch it with thy celestiall quicknesse,
        That it may hang and move
        After thy love.

Then with our trinitie of light,
Motion and heat, let's take our flight
        Unto the place where thou
        Before didst bow.

Get me a standing there, and place
Among the beams, which crown the face
        Of him, who dy'd to part
        Sinne and my heart :

That so among the rest I may
Glitter, and curle, and winde as they :
        That winding is their fashion
        Of adoration.

Sure wilt thou joy, by gaining me
To flie home like a laden bee
        Unto that hive of beams
        And garland-streams.

The Starre

There are eight verses with four short lines each. The whole poem is founded on a conceit; it is addressed to a star - one of the stars that form a diadem round Christ's head in heaven. There is a spirit of gaiety in the poem: Herbert has found a semi-humorous symbol for his fantasy, and he writes it light-heartedly. Vendler calls it a 'jeu d'esprit'. She says: 'It is the sort of poetry he could have written - brilliant, animated, and gay - if his life had been less ravaged by affliction and illness.' She must mean 'could have written *more* of', because The Pulley is another light-hearted poem, so is 'The Artillerie', which is also about a star, and many of his poems have delightful touches of humour.

Verse One.

> Bright spark, shot from a brighter place,
> Where beams surround my Saviours face,
>   Canst thou be anywhere
>   So well as there ?

'Spark' and 'sparkling' are favourite Herbert words. He knows there is nowhere more wonderful for his star to be than where it is.

Verses Two, Three and Four.

> Yet, if thou wilt from thence depart,
> Take a bad lodging in my heart ;
>   For thou canst make a debter,
>   And make it better.

> First with thy fire-work burn to dust
> Folly, and worse than folly, lust :
>   Then with thy light refine,
>   And make it thine.

> So disengag'd from sinne and sicknesse
> Touch it with thy celestiall quicknesse,
>   That it may hang and move
>   After thy love.

If the star does think of going somewhere else, the poet diffidently suggests his own heart as a poor alternative lodging place, but says the star's presence will improve it. Its fire will burn away the dross, especially folly and lust, and will refine and burnish it. He uses the word 'fire-work' and as usual with him, it can have more than one meaning. First, the fire will work its purifying purpose, but also, we realise as the poem goes on, he is thinking of a firework. Fireworks were known in England at the end of the sixteenth century, and Herbert must have seen firework displays in London on his forays to the royal court. The image starts in the second verse as a shooting star coming down to his heart, but then it shoots up again, like a rocket.

The wonderful phrase 'celestiall quicknesse' has many connotations. Quickness means several things: not only speed, but also being alive rather than dead, and also burning strongly: it will give him life, and heat.

The words 'hang, and move after thy love' show that the flight is now upwards, and he is hanging like the tail of a comet, or a rocket, behind the ascending star.

Verse Five.

> Then with our trinitie of light,
>   Motion and heat, let's take our flight
>   Unto the place where thou
>   Before didst bow.

Herbert loves groups of three: here light is God the Father, motion is the son, and heat is the Holy Spirit. All three are also the attributes of a firework. And now, he is joined firmly on to them - it is '*our* flight', rather than, when it came down, '*thy*......' Together they will go up to the place where the star had been attending on its lord.

In Verse Six, as in Verse One, we are given a Blake-like vision of Christ in heaven with beams of light streaming out from his head - the sun and the son are conjoined. And the beams are not static, but are weaving and winding round about his head.

Verses Six and Seven.

> Get me a standing there, and place
> Among the beams, which crown the face
>   Of him, who dy'd to part
>   Sinne and my heart :

> That so among the rest I may
> Glitter, and curle, and winde as they :
>   That winding is their fashion
>   Of adoration.

'Standing' is a many-faceted word. It means a certain place in a hierarchy, and a continuance of existence, and a permanent position. He wishes to be there for ever, near the being whose death saved him.

'The rest'..... Herbert has used this word in different senses many times in other poems. We associate being in heaven with eternal rest, but Herbert wants this rest to have movement in it; he wishes, - a trinity again - to 'glitter and curle, and winde'.

'Winding' to turn this way and that; to encircle; even to blow a wind instrument, such as a horn or trumpet - all these meanings could have been in his mind when he used the word.

Verse Eight.

> Sure wilt thou joy, by gaining me
> To flie home like a laden bee
>   Unto that hive of beams
>   And garland-streams.

It is these last two verses that bring a sublimity to this poem. Herbert is giving us this brilliant description of celestial bodies around the Godhead, but he keeps the humour, in letting us think of his flight up not only as of a comet, but also of a bee laden with nectar, buzzing up to the heavenly hive, which is also both the sun and the Son, and the source of all goodness, and of all sweetness - another quality that Herbert so often blended into his relationship with his God. And the garland-streams we can think of as flowers, flowing as in moving water, continually encircling this source of eternal sweetness.

Vendler suggests that the poem is expressing Herbert's wish to die and go to heaven, but I think he is only expressing a wish to have a permanent link connecting him to heaven during his lifetime. There is no death-wish in it; it is far too elegantly light-hearted for that. Perhaps, though, it has the same childlike humour that Shakespeare gave Juliet, when, thinking of Romeo's death, she said

> Give me my Romeo: and when he shall die,
> Take him and cut him out in little stars,
> And he will make the face of heaven so fine
> That all the world will be in love with night.....

Alas, I don't think Herbert allowed himself to go to the theatre, so may never have heard these lines. But his imagery in this poem is worthy of Shakespeare.

The Pearl . Matth. 13.45.

I know the wayes of Learning; both the head
And pipes that feed the press, and make it runne;
What reason hath from nature borrowed,
Or of itself, like a good huswife, spunne
In laws and policie; what the starres conspire,
What willing nature speaks, what forc'd by fire;
Both th'old discoveries, and the new-found seas,
The stock and surplus, cause and historie:
All these stand open, or I have the keyes:
                        Yet I love thee.

I know the wayes of Honour, what maintains
The quick returns of courtesie or wit:
In vies of favours whether partie gains,
When glorie swells the heart, and moldeth it
To all expressions of both hand and eye,
Which on the world a true-love-knot may tie,
And bear the bundle, wheresoe're it goes:
How many drammes of spirit there must be
To sell my life unto my friends or foes:
                        Yet I love thee.

I know the wayes of Pleasure, the sweet strains,
The lullings and the relishes of it;
The propositions of hot bloud and brains;
What mirth and musick mean; what love and wit
Have done this twenty hundred yeares, and more:
I know the projects of unbridled store:
My stuffe is flesh, not brasse; my senses live,
And grumble oft, that they have more in me
Then he that curbs them, being but one to five:
                        Yet I love thee.

I know all these, and have them in my hand:
Therefore not sealed, but with open eyes
 I flie to thee, and fully understand
Both the main sale, and the commodities;
And at what rate and price I have thy love;
With all the circumstances that may move;
Yet through these labyrinths, not my grovelling wit,
But thy silk twist let down from heav'n to me,
Did both conduct and teach me, how by it
                         To climbe to thee.

The Pearl.   Matthew 13.45.

The quotation from St. Matthew's Gospel which Herbert puts in the title is as follows:

> Verse 45. Again, the kingdom of heaven is like unto a merchant man, seeking goodly pearls

> Verse 46. Who, when he had found a pearl of great price, went and sold all that he had, and bought it.

The poem consists of four verses with nine long lines and a short tenth line, with a complex rhyme scheme. The tenth line in each of the first three verses is an abrupt right turn - a surprise. There is great strength and a feeling of masculinity about the poem: we realise that Herbert is no effete wimpish intellectualised escapist. He has a complete awareness of all the pleasures and diversities of life - of what makes most lives interesting and rewarding. We know he was able to move in the highest echelons of both courtly and academic life, and in this poem he shows how much he appreciated the worth of those worlds. But, as always for Herbert, there is a but.

The first verse describes his academic world at Cambridge:

> I know the ways of learning; both the head
> And pipes that feed the presse, and make it runne

The metaphor is of olives being pressed to produce oil. Herbert's contemporary Oley wrote of 'those horns of oyl, the two universities'; and the word presse also symbolizes printing. Herbert also knows

> What reason hath from nature borrowed
> Or of itself, like a good huswife, spunne
> In laws and policie; what the starres conspire,

He knows about reason and logic - about astronomy, nature, science:

> Both th' old discoveries and new-found seas,
> The stocks and surpluses, cause and history:
> All these stand open, or I have the keys;

He knows many different spheres of learning, which, if he hasn't explored them already, are there for him to unlock and study - a great wealth of knowledge and opportunity which attract him - and then the final short line of the verse comes:

> Yet I love thee.

The word 'yet' makes it clear that this is a turning away from all that richness, to something *more* compelling, that cannot be gainsaid.

The second verse is about his standing in the courtly world of London society. His background is the aristocracy, and he appreciates the worth of this world of privilege .

> I know the wayes of Honour, what maintains
> The quick returns of courtesie and wit:
> In vies of favour whether partie gains,
> When glorie swells the heart, and moldeth it
> To all expressions of both hand and eye,
> Which on the world a true love-knot may tie
> And beare the bundle, wheresoe'er it goes:
> How many drammes of spirit there must be
> To sell my life unto my friends or foes

Herbert briefly sat in parliament. He knew times 'when glorie swells the heart'; he also knew how men's mannerisms change as they scale the social ladder, and, cynically, how everyone loves a Lord. The last two lines show his awareness of what great cost in spirit it is to anyone to remain safe in that worldly environment. (Shakespeare uses the word spirit in the same sense at the start of his sonnet 119: 'The expense of spirit in a waste of shame / is lust in action...')He has no illusions about how power and influence are gained, and knew himself to be in a position to use his family influence to further his worldly status if he wanted to. But then comes the side-step, the turning away from all this:

> Yet I love thee.

The third verse shows his love for all the things that charm the senses:

> I know the wayes of Pleasure, the sweet strains,
> The lullings and the relishes of it

What sensuous words those are! They are Keatsian in their luscious onomatopeoia - not often found in Herbert. The liquid 'lullings' and whispering lip-smacking 'relishes' make us think of deep sofas and plumped cushions, and bowls of creamy syllabub, while lutes and viols murmur around us.

> The propositions of hot blood and brains;
> What mirth and music mean; what love and wit
> Have done these twenty hundred years, and more:
> I know the projects of unbridled store:

These lines are more lively, and are about happy hot-blooded youth - fun, music, laughter, wit, love affairs - all the occupations of healthy young men that have been acceptable back to the time of the Greeks, two thousand years before - and he himself is one of them. They and the next three lines give a clear picture of the man Herbert was: not a stooping pedantic donnish figure, but one who would like to be full of hot-blooded energy and liveliness - strong, aware, alive to every sensation. Sadly he was often ill, but his five senses are all in good working order - 'I know the projects of unbridled store'. I have passions, the same as all men, and resent having to curb them:

> My stuff is flesh, not brasse; my senses live,
> And grumble oft, that they have more in me
> Then he that curbs them, being but one to five:

Then comes the last line again - Yet I love thee.

The last verse is the most profound. In it he explains how, in spite of being fully aware of all the material splendours of the world, he is willingly striking the bargain with God and relinquishing them for something more valuable, like the merchant man and the pearl in the parable.

> I know all these and have them in my hand:
> Therefore not sealed, but with open eyes
> I flie to thee, and fully understand
> Both the main sale, and the commodities,
> And at what rate and price I have thy love;
> With all the circumstances that may move:

He knows how great is the sacrifice he is making, and the price he is paying, and what this will involve.

> Yet through these labyrinths, not my groveling wit
> But thy silk twist let down from heav'n to me
> Doth both conduct and teach me, how by it
>   To climbe to thee.

The silk twist that guides him out of the labyrinth of distractions - academia -worldliness - sensual pleasures - is like Ariadne's silken cord given to Theseus to guide him out of the minotaur's maze in Crete. Veith relates both the cord and the labyrinth to writings by Calvin. Calvin writes that the knowledge of God 'is for us like an inexplicable labyrinth unless we are conducted into it by the thread of the word.' This thread of the word, Veith suggests, is extremely like Herbert's silk twist let down from heaven. The thread is not, like Ariadne's, lying level along the ground; it descends from heaven, and, in Herbert's poem, finally turns in to a silken ladder whereby Herbert will climb up to God.

The poem brims with liveliness, and the last lines of each verse are so typical of Herbert's tactics. He carries us along forcefully, and then abruptly surprises us and at the same time satisfies us. Yes, we think, this is the George Herbert we know and understand. If the last lines were not there it would be an entirely different poet, without the tension and conflict we have learnt to expect from him, and which the poem is all about.

The Pulley

When God at first made man,
Having a glasse of blessings standing by ;
Let us (said he) poure on him all we can :
Let the worlds riches, which dispersed lie,
                    Contract into a span.

So strength first made a way ;
Then beautie flow'd, then wisdome, honour, pleasure :
When almost all was out, God made a stay,
Perceiving that alone of all his treasure
                    Rest in the bottome lay.

For if I should (said he)
Bestow this jewell also on my creature,
He would adore my gifts instead of me,
And rest in Nature, not the God of Nature :
                    So both should losers be.

Yet let him keep the rest,
But keep them in repining restlessnesse :
Let him be rich and wearie, that at least,
If goodnesse leade him not, yet wearinesse
                    May toss him to my breast.

The Pulley

This is the most light-hearted and at the same time most contrived of Herbert's poems, written not so much from the heart, as nearly all his poems are, but from the head. He is entertaining himself with plays on words, especially the word 'rest', and he gives a picture of God as a manipulator, setting out to ensnare the wayward with a stratagem. He is using the story of Pandora's Box as a basis for his story, and, like Donne in his poem 'A Valediction Forbidding Mourning', uses a mechanical device to signify a relationship. Donne uses a pair of compasses to describe his relationship with his wife; Herbert uses a pulley to describe mankind's relationship with God.

To understand his symbol of the pulley we need to visualise two buckets on either side of a support, with a cogwheel at the top and a chain which goes over the cog wheel and is tied to each bucket handle. Mankind's bucket is on the ground and the other in the air. God pours almost all his gifts into mankind's side, so it is even heavier. He keeps 'rest' in reserve. Rest he puts in the other bucket, and it is heavier than all the other gifts. Putting it in the other side is the equivalent of subtracting it, so its weight becomes negative. The weight of it is so great that it swings man's bucket upwards with some force, and he is united with God.

The poem is not profound. There is no talk of love, or sin, or grace, and it is told like a child's story of once upon a time.

> When God at first made man,
> Having a glasse of blessings standing by ;
> Let us (said he) poure on him all we can :
> Let the worlds riches, which dispersed lie,
> Contract into a span.

The first line starts the story. Its lightheartedness is increased by the bracketed words 'said he', which make it merrily conversational. God looks down benignly on his creation, and decides to be generous: he pours on him 'all we can'. He speaks of himself in the plural: his angels are helping. The last line of this verse uses two words that each have several meanings. 'Contract' means to shrink together, to narrow or concentrate, and it also means to enter into a binding agreement.

'Span' means a measurement: that between the outstretched thumb and little finger, and also the length of a man's life, or of a bridge. That one small sentence gives us two separate meanings at the same time- both a narrowing into a small space, and an agreement that can last a lifetime. Herbert meant it to mean both.

The second verse lists all the bounties God is giving his creation. First, strength, then beauty, then wisdom, honour, and pleasure - all qualities to make life attractive, but, apart from wisdom, not deeply profound. There is no word of prayerfulness, of humility, of virtue - the qualities are all worldly ones: 'the world's riches'. Strength is needed to battle with life's vicissitudes; beauty is a surface adornment, honour is important in worldly affairs, pleasure is light-hearted enjoyment.

> So strength first made a way ;
> Then beautie flow'd, then wisdome, honour, pleasure :
> When almost all was out, God made a stay,
> Perceiving that of all his treasure
>   Rest at the bottome lay.

Like Pandora's Box, God's blessings are stored (but in a glass), and all emerge, leaving only one behind. In Pandora's box it was Hope; in Herbert's glasse, it is Rest.

Again there is a play on words. in 'God made a stay.' A stay is both a stopping point *and* a support, and also, a stayline holds up a mast or flagpole.The Shorter Oxford Dictionary gives three meanings 1. A large rope used to brace a mast; 2. A thing that supports, secures, or steadies something else; 3. A stationary condition: a cessation of progress. He used this rich word deliberately, thinking of all its three meanings.

This verse makes it seem as if God had not thoroughly thought through his generous plan, and the next verse shows He has realised that it holds difficulties, in possibly making mankind self-sufficient, no longer needing Him.

Verse three:

> For if I should (said he)
> Bestow this jewell also on my creature,
> He would adore my gifts instead of me,

81

And rest in Nature, not the God of Nature :
So both should losers be.

Mankind would be happy in his worldly state, not needing God, who would also be deprived. He uses 'rest' here to mean 'remain' - a third meaning to add to the two meanings of 'repose' and 'everything else' :

Yet let him keep the rest,
But keep them in repining restlessnesse :
Let him be rich and wearie, that at least,
If goodnesse leade him not, yet wearinesse
May toss him to my breast.

Herbert is enjoying his play on the word 'rest'. In the next line he uses its negative - restlessness. Weariness and restlessness are both caused by lack of rest, paradoxically. The two words 'repining restlessness' as well as being alliterative and musical, hold deep levels of pain. 'Repining'- longing for something, dissatisfied - makes the state God is wishing on mankind cruelly uncomfortable.

The final three lines are almost cynically humorous. God is saying 'I'll get him somehow - if not through his own merit, then through my stratagem of making him miserable', and the word 'tosse' is contemptuous - he is to be tossed up, like a worn-out rag of a creature; landing unceremoniously, but mercifully, on God's breast. It doesn't matter that he is not 'good'; willy-nilly, in the end, through his device of the pulley, God will get him.

Herbert himself knew this restlessness. He knew that it was the restless longing to be closer to God that prevented him choosing a life of worldly preferment, and led him to the calling that eventually gave him perfect peace. The two states of restlessness and weariness are what, Herbert is saying in the Pulley, will eventually bring mankind to God.

The Elixir

Teach me, my God and King,
    In all things thee to see,
And what I do in anything
    To do it as for thee:

Not rudely, as a beast,
    To runne into an action;
But still to make thee prepossest,
    And give it his perfection.

A man that looks on glasse,
    On it may stay his eye;
Or if he pleaseth, through it passe,
    And then the heav'n espie.

All may of thee partake,
    Nothing can be so mean,
Which with this tincture, (for thy sake)
    Will not grow bright and clean.

A servant with this clause
    Makes drudgerie divine:
Who sweeps a room, as for thy laws,
    Makes that and th'action fine.

This is the famous stone
    That turneth all to gold:
For that which God doth touch and own
    Cannot for less be told.

The Elixir.

This is probably the best known of all Herbert's poems, as it is sung as a hymn. Because it is in such simple metrical verse it is easy to sing. We don't know that Herbert meant it to be sung, although he himself was a singer and could well have composed music for it, but his music has not survived.

The version that I sang at school from Songs of Praise only had five verses, leaving out Verse Two. Herbert wrote several versions of the poem before the one we have here. In the first collection of his poems (known as 'W') he called the poem 'Perfection', and it did not have the final verse. He added the title ' The Elixir' after he had added the last verse. The second verse was not in his original version either, and he had a different first verse. Hutchinson says of the poem 'No poem of Herbert's shows better his skill in revision.'

Helen Vendler (in The Poetry of George Herbert) pours scorn on the first verse in the final version. She says:

> "I cannot think of any beginning of a great poem in English so unpromising as the first stanza of The Elixir, which is pure versified catechism, with banal rhymes, an awkward repetition of 'things' - 'thing', and an infantile vocabulary."

Verse One.

> Teach me my God and King,
> In all things thee to see,
> And what I do in anything
> To do it as for thee:

But she goes on to say later:

> 'It takes a long acquaintance with Herbert - his delights, his temptations, and his gifts - to see The Elixir for what it is ..... somehow readers have sensed that one version of the essential Herbert lies here. It is only by knowing the multiple

inventions of Herbert's poetic powers.... that we sense what this sparseness means, and how.... it was the bedrock in which all the luxuriant foliage of his more elaborate poetry was rooted.'

'Bedrock' is the word to hold on to here, and when we get to the last verse we'll come back to it.

As she implies, the first verse needs no elucidation: it is a simple statement of intent. I don't agree with her that it is banal. One of Herbert's strengths is his ability to pare down his verse to the simplest possible words: a modern term for this could be minimalist - no decoration or detail. Every word except one - 'any'- is only one syllable. Such total simplicity is hard to achieve, but done for a purpose, which we shall discover with the last verse.

Verse Two is a little more complex:

> Not rudely, as a beast,
> To runne into an action;
> But still to make thee prepossest,
> And give it his perfection.

This is the only verse in which the metre has a slight variation, with feminine endings to the second and fourth lines. 'to make thee prepossesst' means, according to Hutchinson, 'always to give thee a prior claim.' In other words, we should consider every move, as we make it, is for and because of God, and this will give perfection to the action.

Verse Three is perhaps the best known:

> A man that looks on glasse,
> On it may stay his eye;
> Or if he pleaseth, through it passe,
> And then the heav'n espie.

Mark Patrick Hederman in 'The Haunted Inkwell' quotes Helen Vendler quoting Seamus Heaney about this verse:

> "Vendler is unsurpassed at pointing out where lines might be borrowed. When Heaney said in a radio programme 'I

felt that my first poems were trying to write like stained glass, but that I would like to write a poem of window glass', Vendler immediately spots the connection with Herbert's Elixir."

The verse itself is easily understood. Vendler explains it as his 'consciousness of the crucial boundary between ordinary meditation and original insight ..as a change in visual perspective.' It is a change of focus, pure and simple: to see through surfaces to the intrinsic essence; not to miss, as another religious poet Francis Thompson expressed it, 'the many-splendoured thing', by being too caught up in the material world.

Verse Four:

> All may of thee partake,
> Nothing can be so mean,
> Which with this tincture, (for thy sake)
> Will not grow bright and clean.

All - everything in this world - may partake of this glory. Nothing is too small or too unimportant, too mean, to be left out of the possibility of transformation by applying the tincture - and tincture is in alchemy a technical term for 'a supposed spiritual principle or immaterial substance whose character or quality may be infused into material things.' (S.O.E.D.) The magic formula 'for thy sake' is the transforming agent which polishes and purifies everyone and everything. Herbert reiterates this in 'The Country Parson': 'Nothing is little in God's service: if it once have the honour of that Name, it grows great instantly.'(P.249.)

Verse Five:

> A servant with this clause
> Makes drudgerie divine:
> Who sweeps a room, as for thy laws,
> Makes that and th'action fine.

No explanation is needed for this wonderful idea, which, if we remembered to apply it, would make our most tedious unappetising work acceptable. And what a well-chosen word drudgery is! Herbert knew about drudgery, going about the poor hovels of his parishioners in Bemerton.

Verse Six sums up the whole poem:

> This is the famous stone
> That turneth all to gold:
> For that which God doth touch and own
> Cannot for less be told.

The stone is the touchstone used by alchemists. And the word 'touch' was used, Hutchinson tells us, of testing the fineness of gold by rubbing it with a touchstone; also, of officially marking metal as of standard quality after it had been tested. What God has 'touched' and approved as gold, no-one may rightly reckon for less.

Here, the stone is Vendler's bedrock. The poem in its rounded smoothness is representing the touchstone. Herbert's simple poem, written, it might seem, for children, is itself in its lack of ornamentation and its clarity the touchstone itself, and the bedrock of all his beliefs - it is a foundation stone to build on.

Veith in his appreciation of The Elixer (sometimes spelt that way) quotes Calvin, and it is more than possible that Herbert's poem was inspired by this sentence:

> 'No task will be so sordid and base provided you obey your calling in it, that it will not shine and be reckoned very precious in God's sight.'   (Institutes: 3.10.6.)

The last thing to explain about this poem is the beautiful word 'Elixir' .Herbert's use of it is so typical of him, because it has so many meanings - but two are the most apt for this poem. The first comes from alchemy, and means 'a preparation by means of which it was hoped to change metals into gold: specifically the philosopher's stone;' and the second meaning is 'The quintessence or kernel of a thing.' (S.O.E.D.)

Group Two
GOD'S JOURNEY DOWN TO MAN

In The Bag the poet explains that it is through suffering that God reaches down to us. In The Glance he explains that God's attention towards mankind magnetises us back to him. The poem Redemption is a parable : Christ comes down to earth to visit its sinners and to forgive them their sins and redeem them through his death.

The Bag

Away despair! my gracious Lord doth heare.
      Though windes and waves assault my keel,
      He doth preserve it: he doth steer,
      Ev'n when the boat seems most to reel.
      Storms are the triumph of his art:
Well may he close his eyes, but not his heart.

Hast thou not heard, that my Lord Jesus di'd?
      Then let me tell thee a strange storie.
      The God of power, as he did ride
      In his majestck robes of glorie,
      Resolv'd to light; and so one day
He did descend, undressing all the way.

The starres his tire of light and rings obtain'd,
      The cloud his bow, the fire his spear,
      The sky his azure mantle gain'd.
      And when they ask'd what he would wear;
      He smil'd and said as he did go,
He had new clothes a making here below.

When he was come, as travellers are wont,
      He did repair unto an inne.
      Both then, and after, many a brunt
      He did endure to cancell sinne:
      And having giv'n the rest before,
Here he gave up his life to pay our score,

But as he was returning, there came one
      That ran upon him with a spear.
      He, who came hither all alone,
      Bringing nor man, nor arms, nor fear,
      Receiv'd the blow upon his side,
And straight he turn'd, and to his brethren cry'd

If ye have anything to send or write,
      I have no bag, but here is room:
      Unto my Father's hands and sight,
      Believe me, it shall safely come.
      That I shall minde, what you impart,
Look, you may put it very neare my heart.

Or if hereafter any of my friends
      Will use me in this kinde, the doore
      Shall still be open; what he sends
      I will present, and somewhat more,
      Not to his hurt, Sighs will convey
Any thing to me. Harke, Despair away.

The Bag

In the Bodleian collection of Herbert's poems, 'The Bag' comes just after a poem of greatest possible desolation and despair - 'Longing'; fourteen verses long. (Neither 'The Bag' nor 'Longing' appear in the earlier Williams collection.)

'The Bag' is in direct contrast to 'Longing', and Herbert must have put it next in succession to counteract the feeling in the first one of having been abandoned by God. Very often his angry or despairing poems have a last verse or line that holds some hope or relief, but that is not so with 'Longing': The last verse is totally desolate:

> My love, my sweetnesse, heare!
> By these thy feet, at which my heart
> Lies all the yeare,
> Pluck out thy dart
> And heal my troubled breast which cryes,
> Which dyes.

It is the most despairing of his poems. In an earlier verse he asks

> ...... How can it be
> That thou art grown
> Thus hard to me?

He believes he has been abandoned by God, although he knows he is his child, and is begging to know his love again. If the poems are read in sequence, the next one, 'The Bag', comes as a total contrast, and we read the first line with a sigh of relief. 'Away despair! my gracious lord doth heare.'

Herbert's mood has lightened, and he again knows himself to be loved by God. He realises that Christ has heard his miserable outcry - his sighs and groans ; in fact those very sighs have been like messengers which through the medium of Christ's own suffering will be passed on to God.

The poem, seven six-lined verses long, has three different stages. The first stage is the metaphorical description of Herbert tossed in a boat by storms.

Away despair! my gracious Lord doth heare.
> Though windes and waves assault my keel,
> He doth preserve it: he doth steer,
> Ev'n when the boat seems most to reel.
> Storms are the triumph of his art:
Well may he close his eyes, but not his heart.

There is no doubt Herbert was remembering the story of the storm on the Sea of Galilee (Matthew viii.26) when Christ was sleeping but awoke and 'rebuked the winds and the sea, and there was a great calm.' In this verse the storm does not abate. Herbert implies that God has caused it deliberately: 'Storms are the triumph of his art'. But just before disaster strikes he realises he has not been abandoned. Christ has control and is steering the boat through the raging waters.

The second stage of the poem becomes a story, told in a conversational story-telling voice, and starting with a question; a vitally important question. 'Hast thou not heard, that my lord Jesus di'd?' Then the story of his life and death must be told, but first we must be told how God himself came down from heaven and became a mortal.

Verse Two:

> Hast thou not heard, that my Lord Jesus di'd?
> > Then let me tell thee a strange storie.
> > The God of power, as he did ride
> > In his majestck robes of glorie,
> > Resolv'd to light; and so one day
> He did descend, undressing all the way.

The story is being told as for a child - the image of God going through heaven in his majestic carriage, and deciding to alight from it to visit the earth, undressing as he comes, could come out of a fairy story by Hans Andersen.

The third verse is Herbert at his most fanciful. It is a wonderfully evocative description of how the trappings of God's glory become, as he sheds them, part of the wonders of the firmament. His 'tire of light' - his headdress - and his rings become stars; his bow and spear become clouds and lightning; the sky becomes blue from his azure mantle. Some heavenly beings - angels? - ask him what he will now wear, and he tells them simply that 'he had new clothes a making here below.'

Verse Three:

> The starres his tire of light and rings obtain'd,
>> The cloud his bow, the fire his spear,
>> The sky his azure mantle gain'd.
>> And when they ask'd what he would wear;
>> He smil'd and said as he did go,
> He had new clothes a making here below.

Verse Four tells the story, in six short lines, of Christ's life on earth. A 'brunt' is a blow - an assault He endured them to save us from our sins: he lived for us, then died for us.

Verse Four:

> When he was come, as travellers are wont,
>> He did repair unto an inne.
>> Both then, and after, many a brunt
>> He did endure to cancell sinne:
>> And having giv'n the rest before,
> Here he gave up his life to pay our score,

In Verse Five the story-telling continues. God has come down from heaven and become man; when he dies on the cross he is on his way back to heaven again. Christ, defenceless on the cross, passively enduring, is pierced by a spear which makes a gaping hole in his side.

Verse Five:

> But as he was returning, there came one
>> That ran upon him with a spear.
>> He, who came hither all alone,
>> Bringing nor man, nor arms, nor fear,
>> Receiv'd the blow upon his side,
> And straight he turn'd, and to his brethren cry'd

Verse Six brings the third stage of the poem, when suddenly it is no longer the poet's story-telling voice, but the voice of Christ himself that is speaking. This change of voice - 'prosopoiea: the introduction of a pretended speaker' gives the poem a new perspective and impetus.

Verse Six;

> If ye have anything to send or write,
>> I have no bag, but here is room:
>> Unto my Father's hands and sight,
>> Believe me, it shall safely come.
>> That I shall minde, what you impart,
> Look, you may put it very neare my heart.

The wound in his side, he says, is to become the means whereby messages for God can be brought to him. 'That I shall minde' means 'that I shall look after'. He will keep our messages safe, close to his heart, where the wound is, when he returns to God.

What he is telling 'his brethren' - which means us - is that his suffering has opened up a means of communication with God. His death and suffering, which do not come to an end in this poem, as he is still talking to us at the end with the open wound in his side, will be joined by our own sighs and suffering. The two will meet and mingle together. Verse Seven explains this more:

> Or if hereafter any of my friends
>> Will use me in this kinde, the doore
>> Shall still be open; what he sends
>> I will present, and somewhat more,
>> Not to his hurt, Sighs will convey
> Any thing to me. Harke, Despair away.

'Any of my friends'.... anyone who loves me. 'Hereafter' - after he has ascended to heaven. The means of communication is sighs. Suffering is necessary to achieve union with God. Veith quotes Latimer in his assessment of this poem, to illustrate this point: 'Nothing is so dangerous in the world as to be without trouble.....for our nature is

96

so feeble that we cannot bear tranquillity; we forget God by and by.' (Works, 1: 463 ff) (Veith, page 158.)

Vendler sums up the poem: 'No more than Herbert himself, perpetually assaulted by winds and waves, can Jesus, eternally wounded, change his state. Jesus's response to grief is to put it to use, not to wish it away, and Herbert's lesson is to do the same.' (Page 177.)

The final three words of the poem take us back to the first line again We have learnt, through reading the poem, that it is through mingling our grief s with those of Christ on the cross - through knowing that the suffering we are enduring is one way in which we can join him there, and be in touch with God thereby - that we will be comforted, and our despair will vanish. Suffering is given to us deliberately ('Storms are the triumph of his art'). But through it we reach God. Dame Julian says nearly the same thing: 'Sin is behovely;(which means 'inevitable') yet all shall be well, and all shall be well, and all manner of thing shall be well.'

The Glance

When first thy sweet and gracious eye
Vouchsaf'd ev'n in the midst of youth and night
To look upon me, who before did lie
       Weltring in sinne;
    I felt a sugred, strange delight,
Passing all cordials made by any art,
Bedew, embalme, and overrunne my heart,
       And take it in.

Since that time many a bitter storm
My soul hath felt, ev'n able to destroy,
Had the malicious and ill-meaning harm
       His swing and sway:
    But still thy sweet originall joy,
Sprung from thine eye, did work within my soul,
And surging griefs, when they grew bold, controll,
       And got the day.

If thy first glance so powerful be,
A mirth but open'd and seal'd up again:
What wonders shall we feel, when we shall see
       Thy full-ey'd love!
When thou shalt look us out of pain,
And one aspect of thine spend in delight
More than a thousand sunnes disburse in light,
       In heav'n above.

The Glance

Coming straight after 'Bitter-sweet' in The Temple, The Glance is a happy corrective to the uncertainty of the poem before it. There are three verses, with eight lines each, some long, some short, and a careful rhyme-scheme. The short lines, which come twice in each verse after three long lines, give a special emphasis to the words they hold. The poem has elements of autobiography, describing how Herbert first felt aware, when a youth, of God's power over him.

> When first thy sweet and gracious eye
> Vouchsaf'd ev'n in the midst of youth and night
> To look upon me, who before did lie
> Weltring in sinne;

'In the midst of youth and night' is a strange combination of words, but Herbert, looking back, knows God found him and shed light on him while he was surrounded by ignorance and darkness, and 'weltring in sinne.' 'Weltring' is a great word: it makes me think of squelching mud and wellington boots: Chambers dictionary defines 'welter' as '...... to wallow about in dirt or moral degradation' - and that is how Herbert meant it. But the next three lines give a feeling of awaking from a dream, to find a sweetness enveloping and filling him, as if he has been sprinkled and stroked with some sweet substance like a cordial.

> I felt a sugred, strange delight,
> Passing all cordials made by any art,
> Bedew, embalme, and overrunne my heart,
> And take it in.

The sweetness has entered and overrun his heart, and he is 'taken in'; accepted.

He knows that as a youth God found him, welcomed him, and entrapped him in his sweetness. But in the second verse Herbert tells of the tumult of negative forces he has had to contend with since that time:

Since that time many a bitter storm
My soul hath felt, ev'n able to destroy,
Had the malicious and ill-meaning harm
His swing and sway:

Had the malign forces been able to gain power over him they would have destroyed him. But mercifully the power of the original glance of God is able to counteract this evil force.

But still thy sweet originall joy,
Sprung from thine eye, did work within my soul,
And surging griefs, when they grew bold, controll,
And got the day.

The joy of the knowledge of God's attention to him won the day. The last verse holds the greatest lines, and most especially the last four lines:

If thy first glance so powerful be,
A mirth but open'd and seal'd up again:
What wonders shall we feel, when we shall see
Thy full-ey'd love!
When thou shalt look us out of pain,
And one aspect of thine spend in delight
More than a thousand sunnes disburse in light,
In heav'n above.

When finally he is allowed to see God, eye to eye, when God's look will be of pure love, the light shining out from that look will be greater than that of a thousand suns. Nowhere else does Herbert speak of actually seeing God face to face. And the image of the light of a thousand suns is the most exuberant in all his poetry. He aligns God's glances with joy, with mirth, and, twice, with delight. And the final delight is brighter than a thousand suns. The joy mirth and delight spring from his realisation that God is looking at him; is aware of him - wants him, needs him, is communicating with him. The power is in the eye of God, and it comes to help him 'through surging griefs.'

Helen Vendler in 'The Poetry of George Herbert' says that for her the best line in the poem is 'When thou shalt look us out of pain', because it is so unexpected: we think he will say 'When thou dost take us out of pain'. She tells us Herbert used 'look' because he wished to connect feeling with seeing. The conjunction finally comes in the lines

> What wonders shall we *feel*, when we shall *see*
> Thy full-eyed love!

The Canadian scholar Gene Edward Veith, who writes in his fine book 'Reformation Spirituality' of Herbert being a follower of Calvin, finds in this poem strong echoes of Calvin. Calvin, in Institutes 3.20.11., says:

> '....for the saints the occasion that best stimulates them to call upon God is when....they are troubled by the greatest unrest, and are almost driven out of their senses, until faith opportunely comes to their relief. For among such tribulations God's goodness so shines upon them that even when they groan with weariness under the weight of present ills.....yet, relying upon his goodness, they are relieved of the difficulty of bearing them, and are solaced.'

Veith says of the poem : 'the paradigm suggested in this poem of 'surging griefs' in conflict and finally controlled by 'sweet original joy' is perhaps applicable to Herbert's poetry as a whole.'

The beauty of the poem to me lies in the imagery in the last four lines of the first verse, especially the phrases 'sugard, strange delight' which 'bedew, embalme, and overrunne my heart', and the splendour of the imagery of the thousand sunnes in the last verse.

Redemption

Having been tenant long to a rich Lord
Not thriving, I resolved to be bold,
And make a suit unto him, to afford
A new small-rented lease, and cancell th'old.
In heaven at his manour I him sought ;
    They told me there, that he was lately gone
    About some land, which he had lately bought,
Long since on earth, to take possession.
I straight return'd, and knowing his great birth,
    Sought him accordingly in great resorts ;
    In cities, theatres, gardens, parks, and courts :
At length I heard a ragged noise and mirth
    Of theeves and murderers : there I him espied,
    Who straight, *Your suit is granted,* said, and died.

Redemption.

This is a sonnet, Shakespearean except for the first four lines of the sestet, which tells an allegorical story: it is a parable. Helen Vendler says of this parable: 'Mystification is no part of Herbert's allegories..... they exist to be deciphered easily. And T.S.Eliot, in his booklet 'George Herbert', says of the poem: 'Herbert is a master of the simple everyday word in the right place, and charges it with concentrated meaning, as in 'Redemption', one of the poems known to all readers of anthologies.' This is not necessarily true: three anthologies I have just looked in do not have it. Here it is.

> Having been tenant long to a rich Lord,
> Not thriving, I resolved to be bold,
> And make a suit unto him, to afford
> A new small-rented lease, and cancell th'old.
> In heaven at his manour I him sought:
> They told me there, that he was lately gone
> About some land, which he had dearly bought
> Long since on earth, to take possession.
> I straight return'd, and knowing his great birth,
> Sought him accordingly in great resorts;
> In cities, theatres, gardens, parks, and courts:
> At length I heard a ragged noise and mirth
> Of theeves and murderers: there I him espied,
> Who straight, *Your suit is granted,* said, and died.

The poem starts as if it is one of Christ's parables, except that it is in the first person, which makes it immediate: we are involved at once. Herbert himself is the poor tenant who can't afford the place where he is living, and is needing to find something different. Anyone can work out their own explanation of the parable: to me the meaning is that Herbert wishes to change his life. He decides to apply to his Lord God, to change to a way of living he believes will be even richer and more rewarding, but different .He follows his Lord down to earth, expecting to find him in some 'great resort', and searches for him,

'In cities, theatres, gardens, parks and courts'.

[This line makes me wonder if Wordsworth knew this sonnet, when he wrote 'On Westminster Bridge', with its similar line:
'Ships, towers, domes, theatres and temples lie
Open unto the fields, and to the sky.']

But Herbert's Lord is not in these grand places - he is in the haunts of the worst sinners in the world; not only thieves, but murderers. The next phrase, 'of ragged noise and mirth' instantly conjures up a disreputable bawdy scenario. Here Herbert spies his Lord, who, amongst all the confusion, is aware of what Herbert needs: he grants his suit. But that is not the end of the poem - if it were, it would have no special impact. The shock comes in the last two words - 'and died.' We are shaken by them - hollowed out. Not only has his Lord consorted with thieves and murderers in their loathsome surroundings, but he has given his life for them - and for Herbert too. It is significant that at Christ's crucifixion he was surrounded by thieves and murderers. The thieves were being crucified with him, and the murderers were the men who were crucifying him.

Herbert now knows that his life must be for ever changed. His suit has been granted, which allows him to follow his Lord, and following his Lord means following him to his death. The great Lord has humbled himself to the level of the least of his fellow men, but by his death he gives them redemption, the title of the poem. The granting of the suit and the death of the granter are linked together - one cannot happen without the other.

The strength of the poem lies in its immediacy, and the ending is so unexpected that we again find Herbert's shock-tactics, as in The Sacrifice, utterly compelling. The last line says so much, so succinctly, that one commentator (Professor Moelwyn Taylor) says of it: 'And now you have one of the most marvellous lines that Herbert ever wrote, extremely complex in its punctuation, and...very difficult to read. It's great dramatic poetry......This is the kind of writing which actually catches the movement of human speech.' Again, for me, this poem is one of the finest Herbert wrote.

Group Three
DOUBT AND REBELLIOUSNESS

Affliction autobiographically describes how God surrounds the poet with gifts, and then with afflictions, but eventually leaves him with the realisation that whatever treatment he receives he must still maintain his love for God. The Collar is filled with resentment at the treatment God is meting out to him - right up to the last two lines he expresses his rebelliousness, and then suddenly capitulates. Bitter-Sweet is a cry from the heart of his incomprehension of the suffering God is inflicting on him, through which he will nevertheless continue to love him.

Affliction (I)

When first thou didst entice to thee my heart,
　　　　I thought the service brave:
So many joyes I writ down for my part,
　　　　Besides what I might have
Out of my stock of naturall delights,
Augmented with thy gracious benefits.

I looked on thy furniture so fine,
　　　　And made it fine to me:
Thy glorious household-stuffe did me entwine,
　　　　And 'tice me unto thee.
Such starres I counted mine: both heav'n and earth
Payd me my wages in a world of mirth.

What pleasures could I want, whose King I serv'd,
　　　　Where joyes my fellows were?
Thus argu'd into hopes, my thoughts reserved
　　　　No place for grief or fear.
Therefore my sudden soul caught at the place,
And made her youth and fierceness seek thy face.

At first thou gave me milk and sweetnesses;
　　　　I had my wish and way:
My dayes were straw'd with flow'rs and happinesse;
　　　　There was no moneth but May.
But with my yeares sorrow did twist and grow,
And made a partie unawares for wo.

My flesh began unto my soul in pain,
　　　　Sicknesses cleave my bones;
Consuming agues dwell in ev'ry vein,
　　　　And tune my breath to grones.
Sorrow was all my soul; I scarce beleeved,
Till grief did tell me roundly, that I lived.

When I got health, thou took'st away my life,
          And more; for my friends die:
My mirth and edge was lost; a blunted knife
          Was of more use than I.
Thus thinne and lean without a fence or friend,
I was blown through with ev'ry storm and winde.

Whereas my birth and spirit rather took
          The way that takes the town;
Thou didst betray me to a lingring book,
          And wrap me in a gown.
I was entangled in a world of strife
Before I had the power to change my life,

Yet, for I threatned oft the siege to raise,
          Not simpring all mine age,
Thou often didst with academick praise
          Melt and dissolve my rage.
I took thy sweetned pill, till I came where
I could not go away, nor persevere.

Yet lest perchance I should too happy be
          In my unhappinesse,
Turning my purge to food, thou throwest me
          Into more sicknesses.
Thus doth thy power crosse-bias me, not making
Thine own gift good, yet me from my wayes taking.

Now I am here, what thou wilt do with me
          None of my books will show:
I reade, and sigh, and wish I were a tree;
          For sure then I should grow
To fruit or shade: at least some bird would trust
His household to me, and I should be just.

Yet, though thou troublest me, I must be meek;
       In weaknesse must be stout.
Well, I will change the service, and go seek
       Some other master out.
Ah my deare God! though I am clean forgot,
Let me not love thee, if I love thee not.

Affliction (1)

This is one of Herbert's longer poems, and one of the most autobiographical. It is likely that he wrote it soon after his mother died, in 1627. It has eleven verses of six lines each, and each verse has a pattern of long and short lines, which make it seem informal, conversational - as if he is speaking, pausing, speaking again in a rush.

Herbert wrote five poems called Affliction. The Archbishop of Canterbury, Dr. Rowan Williams, has written a chapter about them in his book 'Anglican Identities', published in 2004 by Darton, Longman & Todd, Ltd.

The poem is addressed to God, and his feelings towards him go through abrupt changes. It is a confrontational poem. It starts loyally: in the first four verses he is cheerful in his initial introduction to service to his lord. But his tone changes as the poem progresses.

The first verse has gaiety in the opening lines, and a teasing, informal familiarity.

> When first thou didst entice to thee my heart,
> I thought the service brave:

Herbert is passive: God has made the advances. But Herbert is happy to have been enticed. He goes on:

> So many joyes I writ down for my part,
> Besides what I might have
> Out of my stock of naturall delights,
> Augmented with thy gracious benefits.

He was happy before, but then his store of happiness was increased.

In the next verse he describes how all the trappings of God's household ensnare him with their beauties, and he uses the (shortened) word 'entice' again:

> I looked on thy furniture so fine,
> > And made it fine to me:
> Thy glorious household stuffe did me entwine
> > And 'tice me unto thee.
> Such starres I counted mine, both heaven and earth
> Payd me my wages in a world of mirth.

His communion with the wonders of heaven and earth and his feeling that they belonged to him was ample payment for his service to his God.

In Verse Three he asks himself a question: everything is so good, so joyful, but there is a doubt:

> What pleasures could I want, whose king I served,
> > Where joyes my fellows were?
> Thus argu'd into hopes, my thoughts reserved
> > No place for grief or fear.
> Therefore my sudden soul caught at the place
> And made her youth and fierceness seek thy face.

His 'sudden soul' - full of startling energy - looks, with questioning fierceness, into his lord's face, to make sure that he is safe in his care. The next verse seems at first to show his reassurance that this is so:

> At first thou gav'st me milk and sweetnesses
> > I had my wish and way:
> My days were straw'd with flowrs and happiness:
> > There was no month but May.

'Sweetnesses' is such a gentle, touching word, and the image of his days 'straw'd with flowrs' is of him walking a flower-strewn path - dancing along it - and the lovely line 'There was no month but May' has the feeling of a simple folk song: 'All in the month of May.' It is all lightness and exuberance: a time of childlike pleasure.The four lines are evocative of carefree mindless cheerfulness. 'Wordsworth captured the same mood, with:

'Bliss was it in that dawn to be alive, but to be young was very heaven.'

But, there is a but. The last two lines break the mood.

> But with my yeares sorrow did twist and grow,
> And made a partie unawares for woe.

'Twist' is a word of great pain. As he grows older, again like Wordsworth, 'Shades of the prison house begin/ to close upon the growing boy.'

The fifth verse is filled with more pain.

> My flesh began unto my soul in pain,

Hutchinson explains the word 'began' by suggesting the flesh in pain at last begins to remonstrate with the idealising soul, and utters its complaint in the following three lines...in the present tense. 'Sweetnesses' are exchanged for 'sicknesses'- a harsh word.

> Sicknesses cleave my bones.
> Consuming agues dwell in ev'ry vein,
> And tune my breath to grones.

He is living again the illness which struck him down at Cambridge: the agues are consumption. The last two lines of this verse go back to the past tense:

> Sorrow was all my soul, I scarce believed,
> Till grief did tell me roundly, that I lived.

As in the verse before, he is 'almost unawares for woe'; in a state of numbness, hardly alive, until shaken back to consciousness by the sharpness of the pain.

Verse Six is a tirade: all indignation and disbelief at the injustice of his treatment:

> When I got health, thou took'st away my life,
>> And more, for my friends die.
> My mirth and edge was lost, a blunted knife
>> Was of more use than I.
> Thus thinne and lean without a fence or friend
> I was blown through with every storm and winde.

He had been well - but illness has robbed him of his liveliness. 'My friends die'; Hutchinson tells us all the friends who died and the dates of their deaths: The Duke of Lennox and Richmond in 1623/4; The Marquis of Hamilton in 1624/5; King James I in 1625; The Earl of Verulam (Francis Bacon) in 1626, and his mother in 1627. According to Izaak Walton all Herbert's 'Court Hopes' died with the first three.

When he says; 'a blunted knife/ was of more use than me', I think he was talking of the sharpness of his wit, which was an important part of his talking and writing, and the metaphor of the knife led him to the adjectives thinne and lean, which in their turn made him think of Pharoah's lean kine, which led to fence - a double meaning: fence as protection from the outside world, and fence as a form of fighting. And he has two images coinciding again- the bare bars of the fence, and the skeletonic figure, nothing but bones, that the wind blows through. This is writing from a depth of uncomprehending grievance.

Verse Seven is the most autobiographical.

> Whereas my birth and spirit rather took
>> The way that takes the town;
> Thou didst betray me with a lingering book,
>> And wrap me in a gown.
> I was entangled in a world of strife
> Before I had the power to change my life.

In the first two lines he imagines how, if he had had his own way, he might have gone to London and lived the life his lineage and gifts fitted him for, at the court. But without his own volition he was waylaid by God into continuing his academic life at Cambridge. He was 'entangled', and his escape route was blocked before he had the power to change his life.

In the next verse he is still angry, accusing God of fatally ensnaring him, and deliberately sugaring the pill with praise for his academic achievements:

> Yet, for I threatned oft the siege to raise,
> > Not simpring all mine age,
> Thou often didst with Academick praise
> > Melt and dissolve my rage.
> I took thy sweetned pill, till I came where
> I could not go away, nor persevere.

There is an ironic bitter humour in this verse - to talk of a siege, and to use the word simpring: he is wryly laughing at his own weakness at being cajoled as he was by flattery. It is this wry humour that so endears Herbert to me.

Verse Nine:

> Yet lest perchance I should too happy be
> > In my unhappinesse,
> Turning my purge to food, thou throwest me
> > Into more sicknesses.
> Thus doth thy power crosse-bias me, not making
> Thine own gift good, yet me from my ways taking.

His bitter ironic humour is even more obvious. Crosse-bias is a term from bowls; when a ball hits another out of line, deliberately changing its position with no apparent gain for itself.

In Verse Ten he is in a quandary. He cannot discover the way he is *mean*t to go; God gives him no guidance. He feels the frustration of being useless, he is doing no good to anyone. Better, he thinks, to have the passivity of a tree? At least then he would be useful, if only to a nesting bird. His life would be justified . You can imagine Herbert's crooked smile as he wrote this verse.

Now I am here, what thou wilt do with me
None of my books will show:
I read and sigh, and wish I were a tree;
For sure then I should grow
To fruit or shade: at least some bird would trust
Her household to me, and I should be just.

Rowan Williams, Archbishop of Canterbury, in his book 'Anglican Identities' has a chapter about Herbert, and devotes two pages to the significance of the word 'just' in this verse, and in Reformation doctrine.(Pp.59-61.) He says: "To become 'just' (to be justified) is to acquire a status, not a role; it is to be regarded by God in a certain way - i.e. it is a 'passive' matter as far as we are concerned." He explains its significance, better than I can, in terms of the theological belief of that time.

In the final verse Herbert attempts a reconciliation, even if it doesn't, to begin with, sound heartfelt. He must, he supposes, be meek, and he must in his weakness be stout. But his rebelliousness has not been completely quenched. The last four lines of this verse are some of the most intensely moving and the most complex Herbert wrote, and the final line of the poem has caused endless critical speculation.

Yet, though thou troublest me, I must be meek;
In weakness must be stout.
Well, I will change the service, and go seek
Some other master out.
Ah my deare God! though I am clean forgot,
Let me not love thee, if I love thee not.

Before I say what I think the last line means, I shall quote some of the other opinions.

William Empson in 'Seven Types of Ambiguity' gives several interpretations.

'If I have stopped loving you, let me go, do not make me love you again in the future, so that I shall regret it if I return to the world. Allow me to be consistent, even if it means an entire loss of your favour.' Or: 'Do not let me spend my life trying to love you, loving you in will and deed but not in the calm of which few are so worthy. Do not make me hanker after you if I would be better under some other master elsewhere, even though this would mean you must forget me altogether.'

Hutchinson says of the line: 'If he cannot hold on to his love of God even when he feels forsaken and unrewarded, he had better not hope to love at all: it is the strongest possible asseveration of his love.'

The writer Vikram Seth, who is now the owner of George Herbert's rectory in Bemerton, gave me his interpretation of the last two lines. He suggested that for Herbert no longer to love God would be the greatest deprivation he could know, and that state of lovelessness would be to him like the deepest darkest abyss of hell.

Helen Vendler, in 'The Poetry of George Herbert' says of the line: 'His life investment - his only life investment - has been in God, and should he leave God, his heart would be entirely empty. Love that has been placed in one hope alone is not so soon transferred.....the absence of love, Herbert realises, is worse, as a suffering, than the loss of health, life, or friends; it would be the worst of afflictions to be prevented from loving. And so his final paradox hastily reaffirms his love and swears that if he fails to love, God may prevent him from loving. In this way, God is re-established as the source of value - value being love - and Herbert's love, his motive for persevering, is renewed.'

Although I find Helen Vendler a most sensitive and penetrating critic of poetry, I find this explanation, while holding much wisdom, too complicated.

John Drury, former Dean of Christ Church Oxford, in an essay written for Reflections to Honour the Bishop of Oxford wrote:

'Herbert calls God "deare". Does he mean it? Should he mean it? The only answer is that an insincere love would be the worst response, that at least God would surely not sponsor that deceit, that hypocrisy. The couplet is a *cri de coeur* from a man caught in the perplexities of that cloud of unknowing which is penultimate existence - and where the only recourse is to the truth of its being so. Things are as

they are and not some other way. And Herbert's refusal to
be deceived makes him a great poet of pain.'

While writing this book, I received a letter from the Archbishop of
Canterbury. In a letter to him I had asked, among other things, for his
explanation of these last two lines.

This is his reply:

'I have indeed tried to interpret that strange couplet in what
I wrote, but still find it elusive. I *think* it may mean, 'Don't
allow me near you unless my love can be sincere - I'd prefer
to be "clean forgot" than to be in a half-serious relation
with you.'

To me, those final four lines are like a sobbing cry - not totally
explicit. The petulant lines:

> Well, I will change the service, and go seek
> Some other master out.

are like the start of his poem 'The Collar' - '.....I will abroad!'
But as soon as he has said them, he knows this action is impossible.
'Ah my deare God!'
This is a cry of total surrender. He knows that he loves God, whatever
God does to him, even if he is forgotten by him.   'Love is not love/
which alters when it alteration finds.' Herbert knows what he means by
the last line, but he has, perhaps deliberately, perhaps from pride, not
made it explicit. He has left out the final telling clause: it is as if he has
choked it back. What he is saying is incomplete. He means:

'Let me not love thee, if I love thee not.....*totally.*'

'Let me not love if I am not able still to love you, *in spite of
all that you have done to me.*'

It is like that perplexing sentence in the Bible, which always seems to
me to be incomplete: 'One day in thy courts is better than a thousand.'
It should have read '........better than a thousand, *somewhere else*'!

Another example, in the New Testament, of vital words seeming to be left out is in St. Mark, Chapter 4, verse 25. Christ is speaking, and says 'For he that hath, to him shall be given: and he that hath not, from him shall be taken even that which he hath.' Hath....what? The capacity to comprehend? Some specific quality was in Christ's mind which would make those sentences less equivocal for us if we knew what it was.

Herbert knows that whatever God does to him, his love must and will continue for ever: that is true loving. And this poem exemplifies this certainty.

The Collar.

I struck the board, and cry'd, No more.
                    I will abroad.
     What, must I ever sigh and pine?
My lines and life are free; free as the rode,
     Loose as the winde, as large as store.
                    Shall I be still in suit?
Have I no harvest but a thorn
To let me bloud, and not restore
What I have lost with cordiall fruit?
                    Sure there was wine
Before my sighs did drie it: there was corn
     Before my teares did drown it.
     Is the yeare onely lost to me?
          Have I no bayes to crown it?
No flowers, no garlands gay? All blasted?
                    All wasted?
     Not so, my heart: but there is fruit,
          And thou hast hands.
Recover all thy sigh-blown age
On double pleasures: leave thy cold dispute
Of what is fit, and not. Forsake thy cage,
          Thy rope of sands,
Which pettie thoughts have made, and made to thee
     Good cable, to enforce and draw,
          And be thy law,
Whilst thou didst wink and wouldst not see.
          Away; take heed:
          I will abroad.
Call in thy deaths head there: tie up thy fears.
          He that forbears
     To suit and serve his need,
          Deserves his load.
But as I rav'd and grew more fierce and wilde
          At every word,
Me thoughts I heard one calling, *Child!*
     And I reply'd, *My Lord.*

121

The Collar

This is an extraordinary poem, and a difficult one. Everyone must try and find their own interpretation. With the help of several academic experts, I have worked out my own way of reading it, and can only offer it as a route map that satisfies me, but may not be an accurate interpretation of the images that inspired Herbert when he wrote it, or the way other people may read it. At least imy interpretation will, I hope, stimulate more thoughts as to its ultimate meaning.

With his usual play on words and double meanings, Herbert chooses a title that can be spelt in three different ways and hold three different meanings. The first is 'collar' - the restricting discipline of a yoke, worn round the neck; the second is 'choler'- the rage that the poet is expressing. The third needs only a slight change in pronunciation: 'caller' - in the penultimate line, Herbert writes 'Methoughts I heard one *calling* ....' The caller is the final mood-changer of the poem, and deeply significant.

The structure of the poem is loose enough to seem randomly conversational, haphazard and arbitrary. It has no verses; it is one long tirade of resentment, each line having a different metrical pattern. The rhyme scheme seems almost non-existent, until we realise that in fact every line-ending does get its rhyme in the end, sometimes as much as ten lines later. It is by far the most freely expressed of Herbert's poems. Elizabeth Clarke in 'Theory and Theology in George Herbert's Poetry' says of its structure 'Even the apparent freedom of that most agonized of poems, 'The Collar' is carefully designed to signify the conflict and its eventual resolution.' Herbert deliberately wrote in this impassioned, abrupt style to express the tumult of his own rebelliousness, only finally resolving it in the regular beat of the last four lines, which settle into calmness after the storm. The poem exemplifies the struggle Herbert endured in deciding whether he was able to subject his will to that of God. The violence of his anguish and his stormy temperament is palpable.

According to his older brother Edward, Lord Herbert of Cherbury, George did have a quick temper: Edward said it was a family trait. In his autobiography, written long after George had died, he said George 'was not exempt from passion and choler, being infirmities to which all our race is subject.' By 'all our race' he probably meant not only his family but the Welsh race, whose quick temper is still proverbial. (Life: pp 12-13.)

Herbert starts the poem violently:

> I struck the board, and cry'd, No more,
> I will abroad!

I imagine him sitting at a table, striking it with his fist and springing to his feet. He has had enough of his own indecisiveness. 'Abroad' can easily, but not necessarily, mean setting sail across the sea.

> What, shall I ever sigh and pine?
> My lines and life are free; free as the rode,
> Loose as the winde, as large as store.'

He is a free man ; there is no reason for him to feel committed to something he doesn't wish to do. 'My lines' make me think of a ship. 'The rode' can be the open road; but it can also be the flight of a wildfowl flying over the sea in the evening. (Oxford Shorter English Dictionary.) 'As large as store': a great cargo of good things to make him happy as a free man. And 'Loose as the winde' again makes me think of a sailing ship.

> Shall I be still in suit?

Shall I still be a paid servant in my master's livery?

> Have I no harvest but a thorn
> To let me bloud, and not restore
> What I have lost with cordiall fruit?

The thorn has been used to bleed him (a well- known remedy in his day for many ills) and the word 'thorn' brings us to Christ's crown of thorns. He has been bled (by Christ's sufferings) to make him well, but given nothing to build up his strength again afterwards - no cordiall fruit.

Sure there was wine
Before my sighs did drie it: there was corn
Before my eyes did drown it.

He has been given bread and wine, Christ's feast of the Eucharist, but through his own lack of grace through his disillusionment with God, they have not provided him with nourishment.

Is the yeare onely lost to me?
Have I no bayes to crown it?
No flowers, no garlands gay? All blasted?
All wasted?

The two near-rhymes, blasted and wasted, thumped out so close together, seem like his fist striking the table again. What profit has this servitude to God brought him? What honours? (The bay is the bay-leaf crown of the conqueror or the poet). What fame or renown has he gained? And the image of the bay brings him to think of a garden, whose flowers have been blasted and wasted by the storms of autumn and winter. He goes on, still thinking of the garden:

Not so, my heart,: but there is fruit,
And thou hast hands.
Recover all thy sigh-blown age
On double pleasures.

There is still fruit to be gathered, still pleasures to be picked up, doubly pleasant for having not had them for that long sigh-blown time.

leave thy cold dispute
Of what is fit, and not. Forsake thy cage,
Thy rope of sands,
Which pettie thoughts have made, and made to thee
Good cable, to enforce and draw,
And be thy law,
Whilst thou wouldst wink and wouldst not see.

All this is addressed to his *heart*. He has made a cage for himself; imprisoned his heart with intellectual strictures. The image now to me is of a ship again, unable to lift its anchor and sail away. But the rope holding it back is insubstantial, unimportant, ephemeral. What could be more ineffectual than a rope of sands? and he has manufactured it for himself with his own 'pettie thoughts'. But he has allowed this rope to tether him, like a strong cable, while his heart was not watching.

Again he furiously reiterates his first resolve to sail away:

> Away; take heed:
> I will abroad.
> Call in thy deaths head there: tie up thy fears.

A deaths head -a skull- is an emblem of mortality. One of his fears of leaving God is that by so doing he will forfeit his immortality. He is saying that he must not let his fear of losing his privilege of immortal life prevent him from leaving God. I like to think 'Call in thy deaths head there' is not rudely addressed to God, but that he is still addressing his own heart about its fears.

> He that forbears
> To suit and serve his need,
> Deserves his load.

Cowardice will weigh him down so that he will never be able to shift this great ship out into the freedom of the ocean and will for ever be anchored in his own discontent.

After all this fury come the last four lines:

> But as I rav'd and grew more fierce and wilde
> At every word
> Methoughts I heard one calling, *Child!*
> And I reply'd, *My Lord!*

As with so many of Herbert's poems, the last lines bring a total change of mood, and a resolution. In these last four lines the irregularity of the metre straightens out into regular iambic feet (the accent on each alternate syllable), and the rhymes become regularly alternate: wilde; worde; child; Lord. Herbert has relinquished his bid for freedom - he has settled back again under the yoke of his master. But those last four lines bring a surprising feeling of relief; of peace after a raging storm. They make me think of the last four lines of G.M.Hopkins' poem 'Heaven-Haven - A Nun Takes the Veil.'

> And I have asked to be
> Where no storms come
> Where the green swell is in the havens dumb,
> And out of the swing of the sea.

An interesting thought on the last four rhymes of 'The Collar' comes in Elizabeth Clarke's book, when she quotes Antony Mortimer (In Words in the Mouth of God.p.40) as saying: 'The crucial words 'Child' and 'Lord' sound so inevitable because the 'eye' and 'or' sounds have been established from the start as the dominant vowels of the poem.' This is remarkably true. In the first ten lines we find these words: I, board, more, I, I, sigh, pine, lines, life, winde (pronounced wined), store, I, I, thorn, restore, I cordiall, wine. Did Herbert do this deliberately,? If so, there is even more carefully organised planning to this poem than we realised, and by such amazingly subtle means does Herbert work his magic.

Veith on page 52 of his brilliant book 'Reformation Spirituality' says of the poem that it is 'the classic example of the collision between the human will's desire for autonomy and the intervening grace of God. The poem portrays the assertiveness of the human will.... the rebellion is not only volitional and moral, but intellectual.' He summarises this on p. 53: 'For Herbert, the self, however much it is scrutinised, is always suspect. The human will is intrinsically in conflict with God's will. Resolution comes with the action of God, with the intrusion of a grace which overpowers or melts away all resistance. Human depravity is countered by the grace of God.'

It is Herbert's honesty, combined with his astonishing gift of language, that give us so compelling an experience of anguish resolving into acquiescence to the will of God, in this his most remarkable poem.

Bitter - Sweet

Ah, my deare angrie Lord,
Since thou dost love, yet strike;
Cast down, yet help afford;
Sure I will do the like.

I will complaine, yet praise;
I will bewail, approve:
And all my sowre-sweet dayes,
I will lament, and love.

Bitter-Sweet

Hutchinson tells us that 'bitter-sweet is used by Gower as the name of an apple.'

The poem is only two verses of four short lines each, but they hold the whole paradox of Herbert's stressful tie to God, and his mournful yet wryly humorous way of dealing with it. Each line holds an antithesis, as does the title of the poem. To me paradoxes seem often to be the carriers of ultimate truths.

Herbert is loved but at the same time punished by God:

> Ah, my deare angrie Lord
> Since thou dost love, yet strike;
> Cast down, yet help afford,
> Sure I will do the like.

A recent book by Geza Vermes, Professor Emeritus of Jewish studies at Oxford, emphasises Jesus's frequent bursts of anger in the Gospels. Herbert knew of these too - but feels the anger pointed at him, in the blows he is dealt; specifically his poor health. Because he is being pushed away, while at the same time being helped, he will show his own resentment:

> I will complain, yet praise;
> I will bewail, approve;
> And all my sowre-sweet dayes
> I will lament, and love.

The poem perfectly typifies Herbert's wry humour: it is drenched in pain, but still has this element of courageous shoulder-shrugging: all right, he is saying, you are intent on making me suffer, even though you apparently love me - *you* see what it feels like: I'll do it to you! The poem shows Herbert's way of addressing God as an intimate - someone he can approach almost on a level; an antagonist in a boxing match; but Herbert is not giving blow for blow; his resistance is more passive. He complains, bewails, laments - but does not strike back. And as with almost all Herbert's poems, the last line and last word give the reprieve. Those last five words hold heartbreak and suffering within their apparent humour: 'I will lament, and love.' In them we hear Herbert's deepest conflict: his stressful tie to God, and his uncertainty that his love is returned.

This poem hangs, embroidered in black on cream linen, in Nicholas Ferrar's church at Little Gidding. It is the only poem there by Herbert. The other hangings are parts of Eliot's poem 'Little Gidding', and a sentence written by Nicholas Ferrar himself.

Group Four
THE ACT OF WRITING AND PREACHING ABOUT GOD

In Dulnesse Herbert compares writing of his love of God to other poets' love poems, and finds himself inadequate compared to them: his own sinfulness blocks his ability to write of his love as he wishes. In the Forerunners he again finds his gifts inadequate to express his love, but realises that all he needs to say is 'Thou art still my God.' In Jordan (II) he mocks his own over-abundant verbosity, realising that all that is needed to express his love for God is 'a sweetnesse ready penned'. In all three poems he stresses that simplicity not complexity is what is needed. The Windows uses the metaphor of windows for the act of preaching about God. Herbert thinks of a preacher as the medium through which God is revealed to the congregation, as are stained glass windows.

Dulnesse

Why do I languish thus, drooping and dull,
    As if I were all earth?
O give me quicknesse, that I may with mirth
        Praise thee brim-full !

The wanton lover in a curious strain
        Can praise his fairest fair;
And with quaint metaphors her curled hair
        Curl o're again.

Thou art my lovelinesse, my life, my light,
        Beautie alone to me:
Thy bloudy death and undeserv'd, makes thee
        Pure red and white.

When all perfections as but one appeare,
        That those thy form doth show,
The very dust, where thou dost tread and go,
        Makes beauties there.

Where are my lines then? my approaches ? views ?
        Where are my window-songs?
Lovers are still pretending, & ev'n wrongs
        Sharpen their muse.

But I am lost in flesh, whose sugred lyes
        Still mock me and grow bold :
Sure thou didst put a mind there, if I could
        Find where it lies.

Lord, cleare thy gift, that with a constant wit
        I may but look towards thee:
Look onely: for to *love* thee, who can be,
        What angel fit ?

Dulnesse

'Dulnesse' is a typically superb Herbertian word, because it has so many different yet appropriate meanings. It can mean uninteresting; slow of understanding; blunt rather than sharp, as in a blade or his wit; benumbed; slow-moving, inactive; depressed and listless; not bright in colour - and every one of these senses fits this poem as a title.

Hutchinson quotes an interesting paragraph on the poem by J.B.Leishman in his book 'The Metaphysical Poets(1934).'

> 'The peculiarity of this poem is not so much that it offers God the adoration of a lover - other religious and mystical poets have done that - as that on Herbert's lips such language sounds perfectly natural and appropriate, suggesting neither an uncommon state of mystical exaltation nor a tendency to weakness or sentimentality. There is that same blend of wit and tenderness which is characteristic of some of the best love-poetry of his age - even that conceit about red and white, which many would find offensive, seems to me, I must admit, entirely in keeping with the whole tone of the poem, and not at all extravagant.'

The poem has seven verses, with four alternating long and short lines. Verse One:

> Why do I languish thus, drooping and dull,
> As if I were all earth?
> O give me quicknesse, that I may with mirth
> Praise thee brim-full !

His poem 'Trinitie Sunday' starts with the line

> 'Thou who hast formed me out of mud....'

Mud --- earth --- inanimate, stodgy, dull. Quickness is life, and mirth is wit, and brim-full means to the top of his bent - with all his energy. This muddy substance that is him needs to be brought to life, and he is asking God to make him live again.

Verse Two:

> The wanton lover in a curious strain
> > Can praise his fairest fair;
> And with quaint metaphors her curled hair
> > Curl o're again.

'Wanton' can mean lascivious, lewd; extravagant in speech; self-indulgent - and Herbert meant it to be pejorative.

'Curious' is a many-faceted adjective. Here it can mean elaborately made; interesting, noteworthy; exquisite; very accurate; or all of them at once.

He is having fun mocking his contemporary love-poets.

Verse Three.

> Thou art my lovelinesse, my life, my light,
> > Beautie alone to me:
> Thy bloudy death and undeserv'd, makes thee
> > Pure red and white.

The first line is like the line from 'The Call':

> Come, my joy, my love, my heart,

which is like Herrick's line

> Thou art my life, my love, my heart.

But this line, with the word 'loveliness', to me is the best.

Red and white are the colours poets give to their mistress's complexion. Herbert gives them to the crucified Christ - red for his blood, white for his innocence.

Verse Four.

> When all perfections as but one appeare,
>> That those thy form doth show,
> The very dust, where thou dost tread and go,
>> Makes beauties there.

All perfections are found together in the form of Christ. The last two lines are about footprints, and to me, the use of 'earth' in the first verse, and dust which is being trodden on, shows that behind the metaphor is the almost hidden thought that Christ's imprint on Herbert's own dust will leave beauties embedded in his substance.

Verse Five holds the wonderfully evocative word 'window-songs'. Hutchinson tells us the word means 'serenade'. Heaney quotes this verse in 'The Redress of Poetry' (p.16), and calls it Herbert's 'impulsive straining towards felicity.....a sine qua non of lyric power.' He goes on: 'for all his sacerdotal fragrance Herbert never fully quelled the more profane tendresse in himself and his idiom.' Heaney finishes this essay on the redress of poetry with a long paragraph about Herbert which starts with the last quotation and ends with the words: 'Herbert's poetry exemplifies the redress of poetry at its most exquisite.'

Verse Five

> Where are my lines then? my approaches ? views ?
>> Where are my window-songs?
> Lovers are still pretending, & ev'n wrongs
>> Sharpen their muse.

'Window-songs' take us straight to his poem 'The Windows.' By window-songs he means the poems, which, like stained glass windows, illuminate and elucidate the glory of God. He has temporarily lost the power to write them. Meanwhile, the love-poets have no problems; they go on 'pretending', (asserting; professing; being pretentious;) and nothing seems to dam up their inspiration.

Verse Six

> But I am lost in flesh, whose sugred lyes
>   Still mock me and grow bold :
> Sure thou didst put a mind there, if I could
>   Find where it lies.

In the third verse of his poem 'The Starre' Herbert asks that the star should burn away his folly and his lust. The first two lines of Verse Six seem to imply that lust is a problem he still has to face. 'The flesh, whose sugred lyes do mock me' sounds like a torment that he does not trust which still has a sickly hold on him.

The last two lines are purely funny - he does know he has a mind somewhere if he could manage to find it.

About the final verse Vendler has a brilliant paragraph:

> Lord, cleare thy gift, that with a constant wit
>   I may but look towards thee:
> *Look* onely: for to *love* thee, who can be,
>   What angel fit ?

'The italicised "look" and 'love" show Herbert doing, as it were, the revision of his poem in public, substituting the tentative alternation for the complacent one. He takes into account our expectation, prompted by his analogy with lovers, and of the word "love," and rebukes himself and us for daring to pre-empt the divine gift. The proper reading of the poem must realize both the silent expectation and the tacit rebuke, as Herbert changes his mind at the last moment.'

We expect him to say 'That I may love and praise thee as lovers do their mistresses.' Instead, he is not so presumptuous: he says that only angels are fit to love God in that way. And he asks God to clear his intelligence, to allow him at least to look towards him with love.

It is one of Herbert's resentful poems; not clearly understanding why sometimes it seems that his inspiration is being deliberately blocked through no fault of his own.

The Forerunners.

The harbingers are come. See, see their mark ;
White is their colour, and behold my head.
But must they have my brain? must they dispark
Those sparkling notions, which wherein were bred?
   Must dulnesse turn me to a clod ?
Yet they have left me, *Thou art still my God.*

Good men ye be, to leave me my best room,
Ev'n all my heart, and what is lodged there :
I passe not, I, what of the rest become,
So *Thou art still my God,* be out of fear.
   He will be pleased with that dittie ;
And if I please him, I write fine and wittie.

Farewell sweet phrases, lovely metaphors.
Bur will ye leave me thus? when ye before
Of stews and brothels onely knew the doores,
Then did I wash you with my tears, and more,
   Brought you to church well drest and clad :
My God must have my best, ev'n all I had.

Lovely enchanting language, sugar-cane,
Hony of roses, whither wilt thou flie?
Hath some fond lover tic'd thee to thy bane?
 And wilt thou leave the church, and love a stie ?
   Fie, thou wilt soil thy broider'd coat,
And hurt thy self, and him that sings the note.

Let foolish lovers, if they will love dung,
With canvas, not with arras, clothe their shame :
Let follie speak in her own native tongue.
True beautie dwells on high : ours is a flame
   But borrowe'd thence to light us thither.
Beautie and beauteous words should go together

Yet if you go, I passe not ; take your way :
For *Thou art still my God,* is all that ye
Perhaps with more embellishment can say.
Go birds of spring : let winter have his fee ;
      Let a bleak paleness chalk the doore,
So all within be livelier than before.

The Forerunners

This is an explosively lively poem, with some of the most expressive and delightful lines he ever wrote. It is because there are so many of these unexpected riches among his poems that he needs to be discovered again by the people who only know the ones set as hymns. This has six verses with six lines each, and each verse ends with a couplet. Like two other of his poems, Affliction (l) and The Flower, The Forerunners is autobiographical, relating to a specific stage of development in his life. In it Herbert is facing the deprivations of aging: he is afraid that as he grows older his poetic gifts are fading.

> The harbingers are come. See, see their mark ;
> White is their colour, and behold my head.
> But must they have my brain? must they dispark
> Those sparkling notions, which wherein were bred?
> Must dulnesse turn me to a clod ?
> Yet they have left me, *Thou art still my God.*

Harbingers has the same meaning as Forerunners : heralds going ahead of a royal party, for instance. Hutchinson tells us they were sent in advance 'to purvey lodgings by chalking the doors. 'The chalk would be white, and Herbert sees this as a metaphor for the whiteness on his own head.He doesn't use exclamation marks, but these three short opening sentences are all exclamatory. It is clear at once that the harbingers are menacing, but at the same time there is wry humour in Herbert's aligning them with his greying hair. This makes it certain that this poem was written towards the very end of his life, as he died when he was not quite forty.

The humour carries on in the next lines. The use of 'dispark' is a play on words: it means to clear out from a park, but also, coming just before sparkling, it can mean to extinguish the spark from his head. He dreads that all his wit is disappearing with age. But he still has the talisman sentence 'Thou art still my God. 'He must hang on to this for dear life, so as not to despair.

Verse Two

> Good men ye be, to leave me my best room,
> Ev'n all my heart, and what is lodged there :
> I passe not, I, what of the rest become,
> So *Thou art still my God,* be out of fear.
> > He will be pleased with that dittie ;
> And if I please him, I write fine and wittie.

He is continuing the metaphor of the harbingers finding lodgings for the royal party. They may be taking over the house, but they have left him his best room, (his heart) which is where he keeps this aphorism, so vital to his continued existence. By 'I passe not' he means 'I reck not..... I don't care..' and by 'be out of fear' he means 'remains safe'.(Shakespeare uses the construction 'I passe not, I..' when Juliet tells Romeo the sun has not yet risen ; she says 'I know it, I.' It must have been a normal means of emphasis at that time.) He doesn't care what happens to his ability to write, so long as he keeps the certainty of his attachment to God. And God will be pleased, and he, knowing this, will feel that his writing is good.

Verse Three:

> Farewell sweet phrases, lovely metaphors.
> Bur will ye leave me thus? when ye before
> Of stews and brothels onely knew the doores,
> Then did I wash you with my tears, and more,
> > Brought you to church well drest and clad :
> My God must have my best, ev'n all I had.

He bewails the lessening of his poetic powers, and is indignant that they should be leaving him, who used them only for holy subjects, unlike poets before him who used their poetic gifts to extol licentiousness. 'Stews' meant both brothels and prostitutes. Herbert seems exceptionally puritanical here, in his condemnation of love poetry. He also uses the description 'well drest' in his poem ' Prayer': meaning 'in good order: seemly.' When he says 'Then did I wash you with my tears' we realise his poems were written from his own agonies, as we understand well from reading so many of them. One of the most poignant verses he ever wrote comes at the end of 'Perseverance'; a poem that he did not include in his final collection sent to Nicholas Ferrar from his deathbed. But its agony stays in our mind, long after we have read it:

> Onely my soule hangs on thy promisses
> With face and hands clinging unto thy brest,
> Clinging and crying, crying without cease,
>   Thou art my rock, thou art my rest.

Verse Four is quoted by Seamus Heaney in 'The Redress of Poetry'.

> Lovely enchanting language, sugar-cane,
> Hony of roses, wither wilt thou flie?

'Such an apostrophe, from his poem The Forerunners, is surely the kind of apostrophe we would like poetry to call from us.' Herbert epitomises sweetness in the nouns he chooses - sugar-cane, honey, roses; and the two lines produce in us a feeling of intoxication - drowning in sweet sensation. We realise how he himself relished this soft lyrical essence in his writing.

> Hath some fond lover tic'd thee to thy bane ?
> And wilt thou leave the church, and love a stie?
>   Fie, thou wilt soil thy broider'd coat,
> And hurt thyself, and him that sings the note.

'tic'd' means 'enticed', 'bane' means 'ruin'. Poetic inspiration dressed in an ornately decorated coat should not go into places of ill repute, where it will be harmed, as will its writer, by association.

Verse Five carries on this condemnatory tone:

> Let foolish lovers, if they will love dung,
> With canvass, not with arras, clothe their shame:
> Let follie speak in her own native tongue.
> True beautie dwells on high: ours is a flame
>   But borrow'd thence to light us thither.
> Beautie and beauteous words should go together.

Canvas was used in clothes then, but arras, a richly embroidered tapestry, was much finer. It is the 'broider'd coat' of the previous verse. Beauteous words should only be used to extol true beauty, which is like a torch sent down from heaven to light us back on high.

Verse Six

> Yet if you go, I passe not ; take your way :
> For *Thou art still my God,* is all that ye
> Perhaps with more embellishment can say.
> Go birds of spring : let winter have his fee ;
>   Let a bleak paleness chalk the doore,
> So all within be livelier than before.

He uses 'I passe not' again, as in Verse Two, to mean he doesn't care if his poetic inspiration leaves him. Let it go. He will still be able to say, and perhaps still with some beautiful language, that God is still his God. The inspiration of the singing birds of spring may have left, and, like the white chalk of the harbingers on the door, winter have taken over his life, but as long as he has his talisman, he will still be able to hold on to liveliness, and, with a sort of despairing optimism, he hopes this will still be so, even when his outward appearance is old and wintery.

Jordan (II)

When first my lines of heav'nly joyes made mention
Such was their lustre, they did so excell,
That I sought out quaint words, and trim invention;
My thoughts began to burnish, sprout and swell,
Curling with metaphors a plain intention,
Decking the sense, as if it were to sell.

Thousands of notions in my braine did runne,
Off'ring their service, if I were not sped :
I often blotted what I had begunne ;
This was not quick enough, and that was dead.
Nothing could seem too rich to clothe the sunne,
 Much lesse those joyes which trample on his head.

As flames do work and winde, when they ascend,
So did I weave myself into the sense.
But while I bustled, I might heare a friend
Whisper, *How wide is all this long pretence!*
There is in love a sweetnessse readie penn'd:
Copie out onlie that, and save expense.

Jordan (II)

In the first (Williams) collection of Herbert's poetry this poem was titled "Invention", and that is what it is all about. 'Invention' was a term used in rhetoric involving 'the selecting of topics to be treated, or of arguments to be used' (S.O.E.D.) Elizabeth Clarke in her chapter 'Herbert and Savonarola' explains Savonarola's attitude to 'invention' telling us it was 'the word which for Savonarola was most characteristic of "duplicitas" .... a mixture of artificiality and human effort that so repelled Savonarola'. What he advocated for religious writing was 'simplicitas' - direct honesty straight from the heart.

The new title for the poem - 'Jordan' was chosen by Herbert, Hutchinson suggests, because of the supposed cleansing powers of the River Jordan. He quotes Kings II. v. 10, where Elisha tells Naaman the Syrian to 'Go and wash in Jordan seven times... and thou shalt be clean.' Herbert wishes to cleanse his poetry of its artificiality, and write simply from the heart. The poem is in three six-lined verses. It is the second he wrote with this title. 'Jordan(I) is also about over- decorated writing, and is a splendid poem too, with such strong lines as

> 'Is all good structure in a winding stair?
> May no lines passe, except they do their dutie
> Not to a true, but painted chair?'

He was railing against a current fashion in poetry, exemplified by an earlier poet, John Lyly in his 'Euphues', which was written in an artificial and affected style, 'with an abundance of antitheses, alliteration, and similes... and high-flown language.' (S.O.E.D.)

Verse One:

> When first my lines of heav'nly joyes made mention
> Such was their lustre, they did so excell,
> That I sought out quaint words, and trim invention;
> My thoughts began to burnish, sprout and swell,
> Curling with metaphors a plain intention,
> Decking the sense, as if it were to sell.

He is mocking himself, caricaturing his early poetic efforts - looking back at them and laughing at them. 'Burnish' can mean increase in girth: swell. 'Curling with metaphors' - making something plain and straight become curly like hair that is curled, complicating and obscuring the original meaning. He uses this metaphor in his poem "Dulnesse':

> The wanton lover.....can praise his fairest fair;
> And with quaint metaphors her curled hair
> Curl o're again.

The last line of this verse : 'Decking the sense, as if it were to sell' means over-decorating a simple truth in order to make it more attractive.
Vendler talks (on p.138) of his poetic debt to Donne, and says:

> He may have taken his conversational immediacy from Donne, but Donne's poems, on the whole, do not teach transparency or self-effacement. These virtues Herbert taught himself.'

She quotes a line from his poem 'Conscience':

> 'My words must come, but like a noiseless sphere.'

He knows that his writing must be direct and utterly simple.

In Verse Two he regrets the haste with which he tried to set down his thoughts, and their over-abundance:

> Thousands of notions in my braine did runne,
> Off'ring their service, if I were not sped :
> I often blotted what I had begunne ;
> This was not quick enough, and that was dead.
> Nothing could seem too rich to clothe the sunne,
> Much lesse those joyes which trample on his head.

'If I were not sped' - if I gave myself enough time to do it. He wrote so fast that he often smudged it, and the result was either not quick - (lively) - enough, or else was dead, and had no impact at all.

'To clothe the sunne' - to describe both the sun and the Son of heaven.

The last line - 'Those joyes which trample on his head' is hard to interpret, especially the word 'trample'. Perhaps the meaning is that too much over-elaboration in trying to express those joys will harm the image: trample on it instead of allowing it to shine. The image of fiery rays carries on into the next verse: the halo of light becomes tongues of flame weaving and winding up from the sun, like wreathes of smoke from a fire.

Verse Three:

> As flames do work and winde, when they ascend,
> So did I weave myself into the sense.
> But while I bustled, I might heare a friend
> Whisper, *How wide is all this long pretence!*
> *There is in love a sweetnesse readie penn'd:*
> *Copie out onlie that, and save expense.*

He is saying his writing was convoluted, and in the centre of the complex metaphors the straightforward truth was hidden. He bustled - hurried in a fussy manner - taking too much trouble over unnecessary details. But then he hears this inner voice. In all his poems, if it is God or Christ speaking to him, he prints their words in italics. So this 'friend' is his lord and master, and his inspiration. And the friend is softly correcting him, and making him look again at his work. He tells him his 'pretence' - pretentiousness and artificiliaty - has been going on too long, and perhaps it is also wide of the mark.

The important word in the next line is 'love'. There is no false invention about that - it is intrinsic in itself, and needs no ornamentation. Find that in your heart, express it, and you will need no more expenditure of unnecessary words.

'Look in thy heart and write' was Sir Philip Sidney's advice in the first of his sonnets "Astrophel and Stella', about poetic invention, and Herbert must have been familiar with this. It conforms, as Elizabeth

Clarke tells us on page 50, to Savonarola's formula of 'simplicitas'. Above all, writing should be simple, and natural. Herbert follows this precept in all the greatest of his poems, and it finds its apotheosis in the last two in both collections : Heaven, and Love (III).

The Windows.

Lord, how can man preach thy eternall word ?
            He is a brittle crazie glasse :
Yet in thy temple thou dost him afford
            This glorious and transcendent place,
            To be a window, through thy grace.

But when thou dost anneal in glasse thy storie,
            Making thy life to shine within
The holy Preachers ; then the light and glorie
            More rev'rend grows, & more doth win :
            Which else shows watrish, bleak, & thin.

Doctrine and life, colours and light, in one
            When they combine and mingle, bring
A strong regard and aw : but speech alone
            Doth vanish like a flaring thing,
            And in the eare, not conscience ring.

The Windows

Herbert used the emblem of windows in more than one poem (an emblem being a symbolic representation of something else, usually an abstract quality.) This poem uses the windows to represent preachers and preaching. It should be read remembering his advice to the Country Parson about preaching, which is Chapter Seven in his 'A Priest to the Temple' which he wrote in 1632, explaining how a country parson should conduct himself and run his parish. In this chapter he describes how a parson should gain the attention of his congregation:

> 'It is gained, first, by choosing....moving and ravishing texts, whereof the Scriptures are full. Secondly, by dipping, and seasoning all our words and sentences in our hearts, before they come into our mouths, truly affecting, and cordially expressing all we say; so that the auditors may plainly perceive that every word is hart-deep.'

This was Herbert's maxim for his own preaching. But being the man he was, full of self-doubt, he wrote 'The Windows' mistrusting his own ability to live up to this high ideal. There are three verses of five lines, each ending with a rhyming couplet.

Verse One starts with an abrupt question:

> Lord, how can man preach thy eternall word ?
> He is a brittle crazie glasse :
> Yet in thy temple thou dost him afford
> This glorious and transcendent place,
> To be a window, through thy grace.

He himself is that 'brittle crazie glasse' - a glass that has not yet been set into a window, waiting, uncut, to be used. He as a preacher has been given the responsibility of being the medium through which the glory of God is to be viewed. And God is the glazier who designs and sets the windows in position.

Verse Two:

> But when thou dost anneal in glasse thy storie,
>> Making thy life to shine within
> The holy Preachers ; then the light and glorie
>> More rev'rend grows, & more doth win :
>> Which else shows watrish, bleak, & thin.

'Anneal' means to fix the colours, after they are painted, by heating the glass. Now we realise the windows are made of stained glass, blazing with colour. Elizabeth Clarke, in her brilliant book 'Theory and Theology in George Herbert's poetry' compares Herbert's ideas about preaching to Savonarola's, and quotes this second verse:

> Savonarola talks of divine discourse as transmitting light: this...means that the human medium should be as transparent as possible. Herbert, however, rejects 'pure' transparency in his poem 'The Windows': the light transmitted into the church by such preachers is 'watrish, bleak, and thin.' Unexpectedly, it is stained glass that is preferred for God's message. The light is refracted through colours (with an unmistakable connotation of rhetorical colours) and through the life of the preacher, so that it is a mixture of divine and human elements that is most compelling.'

By 'rhetorical colours' there is no doubt that Herbert was thinking of his own poetry, as well as his preaching. In his poem 'The Church Porch' he writes

'A verse may find him, who a sermon flies.'

Colourful decorative words are a strong means of reaching a man's heart.

The story of the life of Christ is depicted in the stained glass, and this richly coloured display gives substance and glory to the gospel story. The preacher and the glass should conform with each other - his life must conform to the life of Christ. If it does not, the effect will lose its splendour, and his preaching will be hypocritical - 'watrish, bleak, and thinne.'

Verse Three:

> Doctrine and life, colours and light, in one
>> When they combine and mingle, bring
> A strong regard and aw : but speech alone
>> Doth vanish like a flaring thing,
>> And in the eare, not conscience ring.

What a preacher preaches he must himself embody. Mere words, without example, are like a rocket flaring up in the night and disappearing, leaving no trace behind. Words without example go in one ear and out the other, and do not sound deep in the consciousness of their listener for ever.

Herbert's love of stained glass windows must partly stem from the long years he spent in Cambridge living beside the most glorious stained glass windows in the world, in King's College chapel. His reverence for them shows he was not puritanical in his views on church decoration: they held great importance for him as a means of portraying the glory of God, and preachers should, in their lives as well as their words, do the same.

Group Five
AFFIRMING JOYFUL FAITH IN GOD

Two of this group of poems Antiphon (I) and The Call - are now sung as well-known hymns; songs of praise, which is what they are. They are most people's introduction to George Herbert's poetry. Easter has also been set to music, with others of Herbert's poems, by Vaughan Williams. Prayer is a collection of images, each more compelling than the last, linking the poet to the Almighty through the acts of prayer and praising.

Antiphon (I)

Cho. Let all the world in ev'ry corner sing,
    My God and King.

Vers, The heav'ns are not too high,
   His praise may thither fly:
   The earth is not too low,
   His praises there may grow.

Cho. Let all the world in ev'ry corner sing,
    My God and King.

Vers. The church with psalms must shout,
   No doore can keep them out:
   But above all, the heart
   Must bear the longest part.

Cho. Let all the world in ev'ry corner sing
    My God and King.

Antiphon (1)

The word 'Antiphon' means 'a composition, in prose or verse, consisting of verses or passages sung alternately by two choirs in worship.' (O.E.D.)

This poem was surely written to be sung, and we do sing it now as a favourite hymn. It is all exaltation and exultation - Herbert at his most positive and most joyful. The great chorus is repeated three times:

> Let all the world in ev'ry corner sing
> *My God and King.*

I can imagine him striding out on his walk along the river to Salisbury, singing this across the water, filled with gratitude for his existence. It was not a mood that he could always keep hold of, but how merciful that he could express it so strongly when it was there. The exuberance of the four lines

> The church with psalms must shout,
> No door can keep them out:
> But above all, the heart
> Must bear the longest part.

give us his certainty that there are no limits to the amount of praise that can be shouted; and it is in our hearts that we will always hold this great surge of praise in recognition of the glory of God. It is a piece of music that the heart is singing, and it must go on singing for as long as we live.

Easter

Rise, heart; thy Lord is risen. Sing his praise
    Without delayes,
Who takes thee by the hand, that thou likewise
    With him mayst rise:
That, as his death calcined thee to dust,
His life may make thee gold, and much more, just.

Awake, my lute, and struggle for thy part
    With all thy art.
The crosse taught all wood to resound his name,
    Who bore the same.
His stretched sinews taught all strings, what key
Is best to celebrate this most high day.

Consort both heart and lute, and twist a song
    Pleasant and long:
Or, since all musick is but three parts vied
    And multiplied,
O let thy blessed spirit bear a part,
And make up our defects with his sweet art.

I got me flowers to straw thy way;
I got me boughs off many a tree :
But thou wast up by break of day,
And brought thy sweets along with thee.

The sunne arising in the East,
Though he give light, & th' East perfume;
If they should offer to contest
With thy arising, they presume.

Can there be any day but this,
Though many sunnes to shine endeavour ?
We count three hundred, but we misse :
There is but one, and that one ever.

Easter

'Easter' is written as two separate poems with different metrical patterns. Vaughan Williams set them both to music in his 'Five Mystical Songs'. They have musical references, and are wonderful to sing. The first part is in three verses, with six alternating long and short lines. The second part is also three verses, but with four regular lines.

The first begins

> Rise, heart; thy Lord is risen. Sing his praise
> Without delayes,
> Who takes thee by the hand, that thou likewise
> With him mayst rise:
> That, as his death calcined thee to dust,
> His life may make thee gold, and much more, just.

'Rise heart !' 'Lift up your hearts' is the Sursum Corda in the Communion service, with the response 'We lift them up unto the Lord.' And Psalm 57, the set psalm for Easter, has towards the end, the verse: 'Awake up, my glory, awake lute and harp: I myself will awake right early.' These two sets of words must have been somewhere in Herbert's mind as he wrote this poem. As Christ rises from the tomb it is as if he stretches out his hand, and the poet's heart lifts too. In line five, the poet's heart is 'calcined to dust' - pulverised into cinders - by the grief felt on Good Friday, but now the alchemy of the resurrection has turned it to gold, and made it 'just'. Just can mean 'well-tuned' - perfectly in tune with itself. And this musical meaning leads on to the next verse, which is full of musical reverberations:

> Awake, my lute, and struggle for thy part
> With all thy art.
> The crosse taught all wood to resound his name,
> Who bore the same.
> His stretched sinews taught all strings, what key
> Is best to celebrate this most high day.

The cross becomes a sounding board and Christ's sinews the strings, so that his crucified body creates music, and sets the key for the eventual day of rejoicing. It is a cruel image, but one that Rosamund Tuve, in her superb book "A Reading of George Herbert', tells us is an image familiar to people from mediaeval times. She has two pictures from an early manuscript which show, in one, two men with hammers nailing Christ to the cross, and in the other beside it two men with hammers beating an object on an anvil with a third man holding a harp above it. The text underneath reads :

> 'Christ was stendid(extended) on the crosse
> Als in an harpe ere the strings' (as in a harp with strings)

and

> 'O lord how this faire harpe gaf a swete melody.'

The image is one Herbert uses in another poem, 'The Temper.'

Verse Six:

> Stretch me or contract me, thy poore debter:
> > This is but tuning of my breast,
> > To make the music better.

The first two verses have invoked the help first of his heart, then of his lute to sing praises. The third verse combines these two, and looks for the third element to complete the trinity.

> Consort both heart and lute, and twist a song
> > Pleasant and long:
> Or, since all musick is but three parts vied
> > And multiplied,
> O let thy blessed spirit bear a part,
> And make up our defects with his sweet art.

'Consort' is a wonderfully Herbertian word, combining so many meanings, but the one most apt is that of a group of musicians. With the heart and lute of the two earlier verses we are to 'twist a song' - plaiting strands into a cord - and a chord - made of three parts. The third part is the Holy Spirit .To vie, Hutchinson explains, means 'to increase in number by addition or repetition. The heart and lute require the Spirit, which "helpeth our infirmitie.'"(Romans VIII). Herbert paraphrases these last three words by his 'make up our defects' in the last line.

The three verses combine together to give us a perfectly worked musical metaphor for Easter rejoicing.

Then comes the contrasting second part, with a heart-movingly simple first verse. Herbert had an earlier attempt at this poem, which appeared in the 'W' collection, but this second version is incomparably better.

> I got me flowers to straw thy way;
> I got me boughs off many a tree :
> But thou wast up by break of day,
> And brought thy sweets along with thee.

It makes me wonder if Herbert knew the old folk song :

> I've been a wandering all this night, and the best part of the day,
> And when I come back home again I will bring you a branch of may.
> A branch of may I bring you here, and at your door I stand,
> It's nothing but a sprout, but it's well budded out
> By the work of God's own hand.

His metre is like a folk song, and they are both about a man coming with flowers and branches to celebrate a festival.

'To straw thy way' has resonances of Christ riding in to Jerusalem on an ass, and people strewing his path with palms.

'Thou wast up by break of day' evokes the picture of him found walking in the garden after his resurrection.

The flowers and branches brought to him are the poet's gifts of atonement for his sins, but they are unnecessary, because by his death Christ has already atoned for them. The 'sweets' are his gift of redemption.

The next verse, Veith tells us, means that the very cosmos cannot be compared in glory to Christ.

> The sunne arising in the East,
> Though he give light, & th' East perfume;

If they should offer to contest
With thy arising, they presume.

The heavenly sun is no match for God's son: he parallels the sun rising in the East with the Son of God rising on Easter morning - and one far outshines the other.

The last verse says that no other day in the year can compare in brightness to Easter day.

Can there be any day but this,
Though many sunnes to shine endeavour ?
We count three hundred, but we misse :
There is but one, and that one ever.

Easter is the day of all days - three hundred other days in the year count for nothing beside this one, whose radiance lasts for ever.

Herbert wrote two other poems about Easter: one, Easter Wings, he famously wrote with the words on the page making the shape of wings. The other he called 'The Dawning.' Neither, for me, compares with this one.

Prayer (I)

Prayer the Churches banquet, Angels age,
Gods breath in man returning to his birth,
The soul in paraphrase, heart in pilgrimage,
The Christian plummet sounding heav'n and earth;
Engine against th'Almightie, sinners towre,
Reversed thunder, Christ-side-piercing spear,
The six-daies world transposing in an houre,
A kind of tune, which all things heare and fear;
Softnesse, and peace, and joy, and love, and blisse,
Exalted Manna, gladnesse of the best,
Heaven in ordinarie, man well drest,
The milkie way, the bird of Paradise,
Church-bels beyond the starres heard, the souls bloud,
The land of spices; something understood.

Prayer

Prayer, a sonnet, is made up of a series of diverse metaphors, which, like so many of Herbert's poems, swing in mood from a conventional description of his relationship to his maker, through feelings of rebellion, then to a wonderful sweep upwards to a sort of ecstasy, and finally back again to calm philosophical acceptance.

It is possible to watch his train of thought - how one image leads him on to think of the next. But this doesn't make the images he chooses any the less surprising, and therefore delightful. It is a poem rich in imagination, and sprightly in its variety. The easy way to appreciate it is to look at each metaphor, and how it leads on to the next. Here are some interpretations, but everyone may have their own.

Prayer, the Churches banquet, Angels age,

He starts with a flourish - a banquet is a splendid feast; an elaborate celebration, lavishly generous - nothing stinted. At a heavenly banquet angels will be the helpers, and they are ageless, immortal beings, in heaven throughout time. Prayer is thus a magnificent communion with heavenly beings provided by the Church.

Gods breath in man returning to his birth,

At our birth God breathes into us to give us our life: before that we are part of the eternal world of angels. Our breath sustains us, and so does prayer, linking us to our maker, and praying is as natural as breathing.

The soul in paraphrase, heart in pilgrimage,

Hutchinson explains this by saying 'a paraphrase clarifies by expansion'. As we pray our soul enlarges, just as we grow from our birth. And our whole life is a pilgrimage towards God, helped on by prayer.

The Christian plummet sounding heav'n and earth;

A plummet can mean two different things: first, a plumb line to measure distances - Herbert thinks of the pilgrimage, and how far he has to travel, by means of prayer, from earth to heaven. But it can also mean 'a ball or lump of lead, especially one used as a missile' (S.O.E.D.) and this meaning leads Herbert on to his next two lines, where his mood has suddenly become belligerent:

> Engine against th' Almightie, sinners towre,

Herbert is remembering the fierce tirades he has sent up to God while praying; he describes these in his poem 'Artillerie' Verse 3, when he says "We are shooters both....shunne not my arrows". The sinners' tower is a place of defence where a sinner can hide: praying can be a form of self-justifying defence.

> Reversed thunder, Christ side-piercing spear,

He is throwing thunderbolts back at God now, and the most telling image he can think of for man's cruelty to God is the spear-thrust into Christ's side at his crucifixion. Vendler calls this 'the traditional image on which the entire poem hinges.'

> The six-daies world transposing in an houre,

Hutchinson suggests this line means 'an hour of prayer may affect a universe which took six days to set in motion.' Vendler suggests 'an infusion transforming the workaday world into the Sabbath.' My suggestion connects the creation of the world by God in six days to the death of Christ, when the whole meaning of creation was upturned, in that last hour. I also think of the sentence in the garden of Gethsemane:

'What, could ye not watch with me one hour?' Our shortcomings caused the greatest tragedy in history. Another meaning could be that time is irrelevant to God: he could as easily have created the world in an hour as in six days, and in prayer, time has the same irrelevance. But this to me is the hardest line to interpret in the poem.

> A kinde of tune, which all things heare and fear;

This connects for me with the last suggestion for the line before: the intimation of timelessness connects to the heavenly harmony of the music of the spheres. The fear is the fear of awe - the music is there to be heard by all creation, and links up with the mystical sensation that can come through prayer and meditation.

These last two lines lead away from the angry prayers, and into a sort of ecstasy:

> Softnesse, and peace, and joy, and love, and blisse,

He has been transported to an almost tangible heaven, and is in the stratosphere:

> Exalted Manna, gladness of the best,
> Heaven in ordinarie, man well drest,

From there benefits are falling on us; heaven is in order, and man is also in order: they are in harmony with each other because they are in contact through the blessings showering down from above.

> The milkie way, the bird of Paradise,

If these images were set to music they would sound like the end of Beethoven's last piano sonata, Opus 111 - a climbing up into a suspended sphere above all material life; a recognition of immortality among the stars.

> Church-bels beyond the starres heard, the soul's bloud,
> The land of spices; something understood.

The land of spices is somewhere you sail to beyond the furthest horizon . These last six lines show me that in praying and meditating Herbert lifted off from temporal living . They show him to have had experiences of transcendence, such as mystics have. He is not thought of as a mystic, but this sonnet describes in unmistakable imagery the apprehensions of a mystic.

When the vision is past, he comes back into his normal consciousness with new comprehension - the certainty of knowing, once and for all and for ever, that this blissful experience, created through prayer, is reality. For me this poem tells us more about Herbert's transcendental experiences than any other.

The Call

Come, my Way, my Truth, my Life:
Such a Way, as gives us breath,
Such a Truth, as ends all strife:
Such a Life, as killeth death.

Come, my Light, my Feast, my Strength:
Such a Light, as shows a feast:
Such a Feast, as mends in length:
Such a Strength, as makes his guest.

Come, my Joy, my Love, my Heart:
Such a Joy, as none can move:
Such a Love, as none can part:
Such a Heart, as joyes in Love.

The Call

Come, my Way, my Truth, my Life:
Such a Way, as gives us breath:
Such a Truth, as ends all strife:
Such a life, as killeth death.

This, again, is sung as a hymn - but the trouble with hymn-singing is that the words become familiar without the sense seeping through: these words are usually sung to a jolly rollicking tune, and they trip off the tongue as a sort of chant, or spell, and the subtlety is lost.

This is one of the most rigorously structured of Herbert's poems. The shape could be thought to constrict his inspiration, but if we think of Wordsworth's sonnet addressed to the sonnet we understand that sometimes poets like restrictions: it begins

Nuns fret not at their convent's narrow room

and has the lines

'twas pastime to be bound
Within the sonnet's scanty plot of ground.

Sometimes the discipline of a narrow scope can concentrate the mind and produce a condensation of thought that is an essence: it has been strained to a perfect simplicity, all dross discarded. That has happened with this poem.

Herbert has chosen to use words of only one syllable. There is only one word - 'killeth' - in the first verse, with two. Next, he has chosen to start each verse with the word 'Come' followed by three nouns, and the three following lines in each verse start with 'Such a...', and amplify the three nouns of the first line.

The Call is an invocation. The first line is based on Christ's sentence in St. John's Gospel, Chapter 14, verse 6:

'Jesus saith unto him 'I am the way, the truth and the life:
no man cometh unto the father, but by me.'

The Way is our inspiration. Truth cannot be denied or gainsaid; the Life Christ offers us is immortal.

Verse Two

> Come, my Light, my Feast, my Strength:
> Such a Light, as shows a feast:
> Such a Feast, as mends in length:
> Such a Strength, as makes his guest.

Christ said 'I am the light of the world', and he also said 'I am the living bread'. At the Last Supper he asked his disciples to take part in a feast, which gets better through time, and would bind him and all men to him in strength. We can also find echoes of the wedding feast in Canaan, when by turning the water into wine Christ made the feast continue better than before. And again, we can think of his parables of the feast to which the host asked ' the poor, and the maimed, and the halt and the blind' to be his guests, which Herbert recalls in his last poem, 'Love (lll)'.

The third verse is the most sublime of the three:

> Come, my Joy, my Love, my Heart:
> Such a Joy, as none can move:
> Such a Love, as none can part:
> Such a Heart, as joyes in love.

He brilliantly combines the three nouns of the first line of this verse in the last line of the poem.

Robert Herrick in one of his poems echoes this last verse:

> Thou art my life, my love, my heart,
> The very eyes of me,
> And hast command of every part
> To live and die for thee.

Herrick was born two years before Herbert, but lived on for forty one years after Herbert's death. He must have read Herbert's poems, which were first published in 1633, the year Herbert died, and perhaps unconsciously copied this one. The difference is that while Herbert's is addressed to God, Herrick's is addressed 'To Anthea, who may command him anything.' Herrick was also a clergyman, but unlike Herbert, did not keep his love poetry only for God. The last verse of 'The Call' is a perfect declaration of love .

Group Six
THE POET'S RELATIONSHIP WITH GOD

In three of these poems Dialogue, Heaven, and Love (III) - God is given a voice to respond to the poet's questioning and doubts. (In 'Heaven' the voice is perhaps that of Holy Scripture.) In The Flower, Herbert describes his relationship with God in terms of flowers which are affected by the changing seasons. It ends on a note of humble recognition and acceptance of what God has planned for him. In Gratefulnesse he begs God to give him a thankful heart, so that he may always be aware of the benefits he has been given. Heaven is a stylised echo poem. The echo is perhaps the voice of Holy Scripture, guiding the poet towards heaven through the words of the Bble. Love (III) describes God's beneficence towards man: in spite of all his flaws and shortcomings he is welcomed by God to his eternal banquet.

Dialogue

Sweetest Saviour, if my soul
   Were but worth the having,
Quickly should I then controll
   Any thought of waving.
But when all my care and pains
Cannot give the name of gains
To thy wretch so full of stains
What delight or hope remains?

What, Child, is the ballance thine
   Thine the poise and measure ?
If I say, Thou shalt be mine;
   Finger not my treasure.
What the gains in having thee
Do amount to, onely he,
Who for man was sold, can see;
That transferr'd th'accounts to me.

But as I can see no merit
   Leading to this favour:
So the way to fit me for it
   Is beyond my savour.
As the reason then is thine;
So the way is none of mine:
I disclaime the whole designe:
Sinne disclaims and I resigne.

That is all, if that I could
   Get without repining;
And my clay, my creature, would
   Follow my resigning:
That as I did freely part
With my glorie and desert,
Left all joyes to feel all smart --- ---
      Ah! no more: thou break'st my heart.

Dialogue

This poem is of such importance in helping us to understand Herbert that academics and theologians have written many pages about it. The latest to do so is Rowan Williams, Archbishop of Canterbury, in his chapter on Herbert in his new book 'Anglican Identities'. I have used his commentary to help me elucidate the poem's complexities.

It is written as a dialogue between the poet and Christ his saviour. Each has an alternate verse. There are four eight-lined verses, with the last four lines in each having the same rhyme. In other poems Herbert sometimes gives speech to either God or Christ, and it is a way of showing how close is his sense of involvement with his creator - we get the feeling that this dialogue is part of Herbert's every conscious moment, and nearly always it is about his own unworthiness to be considered loved by God.

First verse:

> Sweetest Saviour, if my soul
>   Were but worth the having,
> Quickly then should I controll
>   Any thought of waving.
> But when all my care and pains
> Cannot give the name of gains
> To thy wretch so full of stains
> What delight or hope remains?

'Waving' has more than one meaning.It can mean 'vacillating', or wavering, or 'waiving' as in a legal sense, meaning 'declining an offer'. Hutchinson paraphrases the verse:

> 'If I thought my soul worth thy having, I would not hesitate
> to surrender it, but since all my care cannot give it worth
> (gains), how can I expect thee to benefit by acquiring it?'

For me however the 'delight or hope' in the last line are Herbert's own - he is expressing despair that in spite of all his efforts, he is still, in his own eyes, a hopeless case.

Williams suggests that the first line is reminiscent of the first line of Donne's Song: 'Sweetest love, I do not go For weariness of thee....' - a secular poem to his love, saying that though he thinks they must part, they will in spirit 'ne'er parted be.' Herbert loved to write of the 'sweetness' of God; if he knew Donne's poem I think the similarity was subconscious, for the content is so different; unless it was in deliberate contrast to show that his love poetry was not to a mortal but an immortal being.

Verse Two is Christ's forthright reply. His tone is peremptory, but kind. He calls the poet 'child', which shows, as in 'Love (III)', his fatherly attitude to a less wise, dependent creature. his words are printed in italics.

> *What, Child, is the ballance thine*
> *Thine the poise and measure ?*
> *If I say, Thou shalt be mine;*
> *Finger not my treasure.*
> *What the gains in having thee*
> *Do amount to, onely he,*
> *Who for man was sold, can see;*
> *That transferr'd th'accounts to me.*

He asks if the poet thinks *he* holds justice's weighing scales? It is for me to decide, he says, and if I say I want you, don't start quibbling about your worth: 'Finger not my treasure'- don't look a gift horse in the mouth! I am the one who knows what it means to me to gain your soul, because I am the one who made the bargain to buy it with my death.

Herbert is not convinced ; he argues back fiercely in Verse Three:

> But as I can see no merit
> Leading to this favour:
> So the way to fit me for it
> Is beyond my savour.
> As the reason then is thine;
> So the way is none of mine:
> I disclaime the whole designe:
> Sinne disclaims and I resigne.

179

He himself cannot see his own worth. It is beyond his 'savour' - his understanding, perception. He talks of 'the way', which makes us think of Christ's words 'I am the way, the truth and the life.' And is there the hint of double meaning, with the word 'savour' and the 'saviour' of the first line of the poem? The line could also mean 'It is beyond the skill of my saviour to make me fit.' But as the idea is Christ's, not his, he will bear no responsibility for the transaction.

Williams says of this last line ' The rather puzzling line 'Sinne disclaims and I resign' may be another deliberately ambiguous statement.' But he goes on to a long and brilliant analysis of possible meanings, ending - 'I suggest that he is saying: 'That I should "resign" is exactly what God wants, because such an act mirrors God's own activity.' (By allowing himself to be crucified.)

My explanation of these last two lines is : 'I am not responsible for your decision - although I know my sin makes me totally unworthy of you, I passively resign my will to yours.' We can imagine an exasperated sigh: - 'Oh all right! Have it your own way!' It means that the poet is now Christ's, without any reservations left. And this is what Christ wants. In Verse Four he shows his pleasure:

> *That is all, if that I could*
> *Get without repining;*
> *And my clay, my creature, would*
> *Follow my resigning.*
> *That as I did freely part*
> *With my glorie and desert,*
> *Left all joyes to feel all smart* -- --
> Ah! no more: thou break'st my heart.

To me this verse means 'That is all I want, your resigning your will to mine; as long as you are doing it wholeheartedly and with no regrets (no repining). I made you; you are my creature made by me, and it is right that you should follow my example and resign your will to God, as I did. I gave up my glory, my just deserts; I left all joy, and felt bitter smarting pain.....'

This is too much for Herbert. He cannot bear any further reminder of what Christ suffered for his sake. He interrupts, with a cry of agony.

And the breaking of his heart is the final surrender of himself. He now belongs entirely to God, both his will and his heart, whether worthy or not, and it is due to the sacrifice Christ made for him on the cross.

The last line is remarkable in its abruptness. It is one of Herbert's characteristics, to have a tremendous punch in the last line, which makes us gasp with shock. This gives the poems where he does this the effect of an actual confrontation with him - the words jump off the page and electrify us with their immediacy. It is one of the ways in which the poems become contemporary - as if they have only just been written, and we feel as if we are completely in touch with their writer, because he leaves us with this direct, natural, exclamation, as if he is in the room with us. This is one of the reasons why he is still a living poet.

Gratefulnesse.

Thou that hast giv'n so much to me,
Give one thing more, a gratefull heart.
See how the beggar works on thee
        By art.

He makes thy gifts occasion more,
And sayes, If he in this be crost,
All thou hast giv'n him heretofore
        Is lost.

But thou didst reckon, when at first
Thy word our hearts and hands did crave,
What it would come to at the worst
        To save.

Perpetuall knockings at thy doore,
Tears sullying thy transparent rooms,
Gift upon gift, much would have more,
        And comes.

This notwithstanding, thou wentst on,
And didst allow us all thy noise:
Nay, thou hast made a sigh and grone
        Thy joyes.

Not that thou hast not still above
Much better tunes, than grones can make;
But that these country-aires thy love
        Did take.

Wherefore I crie, and crie again;
And in no quiet canst thou be,
Till I a thankfull heart obtain
        Of thee.

Not thankfull, when it pleaseth me;
As if thy blessings had spare days:
But such a heart, whose pulse may be
        Thy praise.

Gratefulness

I first met this eight-versed poem in an anthology which printed only the first two lines of the first verse, then the whole of the last verse, putting them together to make a perfect small poem about giving thanks to God. As such it makes a fine Grace to say, even if not out loud.

> Thou that hast giv'n so much to me,
> Give one thing more, a gratefull heart.........
> Not thankfull, when it pleaseth me;
> As if thy blessings had spare days:
> But such a heart, whose pulse may be
> > Thy praise.

There is such humour in the lines:

> 'Not thankfull when it pleaseth me
> As if thy blessings had spare days'.

Not only being grateful from time to time, when we remember, as if God too sometimes takes the day off from providing blessings. The last lines describe the strong impulse of registering a rhythm of praise with every heartbeat, so that it is an intrinsic part of our very existence.

Those lines are enough to give us the essence of the poem, and of Herbert's sense of indebtedness to God: it is not a sentiment that he often expresses. The centre of the poem between these two extremes merely amplifies his need to give thanks.

He, 'the beggar', is continually importuning for more gifts, but says that if on top of them the gift of a grateful heart is not forthcoming, the ones already given will be of no use.

> He makes thy gifts occasion more,
> And sayes, If he in this be crost,
> All thou hast giv'n him heretofore
> > Is lost.

But, says Herbert, God knew what he was taking on when he first decided that he wanted our hearts and hands in his service:

> But thou didst reckon, when at first
> Thy word our hearts and hands did crave,
> What it would come to at the worst
>   To save.
> Perpetuall knockings at thy doore,
> Tears sullying thy transparent rooms,
> Gift upon gift, much would have more,
>   And comes.

God was going to have to put up with endless importuning: 'Much would have more' comes from an English proverb 'The much ever runs to the more.' The more we get the more we want.

But God went on giving, and endured the groaning importunity of the beggars, even apparently pleased to hear them, while being used to far more musical sounds.

> This notwithstanding, thou wentst on,
> And did allow us all our noise:
> Nay, thou hast made a sigh and grone
>   Thy joyes.
> Not that thou hast not still above
> Much better tunes, than grones can make;
> But that these countrey-aires thy love
>   Did take.

No-one can miss the humour of those two verses, mocking his own inadequate musical pleadings. But the next verse is much more poignant:

> Wherefore I crie, and crie again;
> And in no quiet canst thou be,
> Till I a thankfull heart obtain
>   Of thee.

On top of all the other gifts, he cannot allow God peace and quiet until he has given him the most important final gift: a thankful heart. And this brings us on to the last verse I quoted at the beginning.

It is, apart from the verse above with its plaintive 'Therefore I crie and crie again' a light-hearted poem, with a sense of fun. But - "And in no quiet canst thou be' lightens that verse too, with its sense of annoying persistence. Herbert is giving God a bad time, and making no bones about it, to get what he wants. It is no good being given all the wonderful benefits God provides unless he also adds on the ability to recognise this beneficence and give thanks for it with every single beat of his heart.

The Flower

How fresh, O Lord, how sweet and clean
Are thy returns! ev'n as the flow'rs in spring;
    To which, besides their own demean,
The late-past frosts tributes of pleasure bring,
        Grief melts away
        Like snow in May,
As if there were no such cold thing.

    Who would have thought my shrivel'd heart
Could have recover'd greennesse? It was gone
    Quite underground ; as flowers depart
To see their mother-root, when they have blown;
        Where they together
        All the hard weather,
Dead to the world, keep house unknown.

    These are thy wonders, Lord of power,
Killing and quickning, bringing down to hell
    And up to heaven in an houre ;
Making a chiming of a passing-bell.
        We say amisse,
        This or that is:
Thy word is all, if we could spell.

    O that I once past changing were,
Fast in thy Paradise, where no flower can wither !
    Many a spring I shoot up fair;
Offring at heav'n, growing and groning thither :
        Nor doth my flower
        Want a spring showre,
My sinnes and I joining together.

But while I grow in a straight line,
Still upwards bent, as if heav'n were mine own,
   Thy anger comes, and I decline :
What frost to that ? what pole is not the zone,
                  Where all things burn,
                  When thou dost turn,
      And the least frown of thine is shown ?

      And now in age I bud again,
After so many deaths I live and write ;
   I once more smell the dew and rain,
And relish versing : O my onely light
                  It cannot be
                  That I am he
      On whom thy tempests fell all night.

      These are thy wonders, Lord of love,
To make us see we are but flowers that glide :
   Which when we once can finde and prove,
Thou hast a garden for us, where to bide.
                  Who would be more,
                  Swelling through store,
      Forfeit their Paradise by their pride.

The Flower

The Flower has a uniquely complex verse form. The first and third lines have eight syllables; the second and fourth have ten, and then there is a surprising little couplet for lines five and six which only have four syllables, and the final seventh line has eight. The little couplet adds simplicity and lightness to each verse, like a nursery rhyme. Herbert keeps this pattern meticulously throughout the seven verses of the poem, and the last line rhymes each time with the second and fourth lines, which gives each verse a satisfying roundness.It is the only poem with this verse form - but he seldom used the same form twice, delighting in endless variations.

There are so many beauties in this poem. The language he uses is that of a natural conversation - fresh and vivid. Because we are aware of his love of double meanings for words we are inclined to look for them all the time - in the title of this poem, for instance. 'The Flower' could mean not only a garden plant, but, differently pronounced, a flow of liquid. There are suggestions of this here and there in the poem - enough to make the suggestion a possibility. For instance, the first line with its three adjectives could as easily be about a stream as about a new season - spring. And the word 'spring' has watery connotations. But it isn't important to dwell on this, although it adds an extra possible dimension, as do all his double meanings.

> How fresh, O Lord, how sweet and clean
> Are thy returns! ev'n as the flow'rs in spring;
> To which, besides their own demean,
> The late-past frosts tributes of pleasure bring,
> Grief melts away
> Like snow in May,
> As if there were no such cold thing.

'Demean' Hutchinson tells us, relates both to demeanour and demesne.

The winter is over; the spring has returned: the frosts have gone and grief is gone too - forgotten. And the last line of eight strong single syllable words seems to give emphasis to this happy certainty. God has organised, as he always does, the cycle of seasonal renewal, and Herbert relates this to his own feeling of being back in God's favour. He has been sadly out of favour.

The second verse gives us his feeling of renewed life:

> Who would have thought my shrivel'd heart
> Could have recover'd greennesse? It was gone

He might be having a conversation_- 'Who would have thought it?' - a sentence anyone might casually say. And 'greennesse' is wonderful shorthand for renewal of life-giving sap. That sentence is striking in its immediacy.

> It was gone
> Quite underground; as flowers depart
> To see their mother-root, when they have blown;
> Where they together
> All the hard weather,
> Dead to the world, keep house unknown.

Herbert is aware of the habits of plants that die back in winter and disappear altogether as if they really are dead, but the imagery in this verse is not harsh - it is as if the plant is a hibernating animal tucked up with its mother 'keeping house'.

In Verse Three he marvels at the contradictory impulses of God:

> These are thy wonders, Lord of power,
> Killing and quickening, bringing down to hell
> And up to heaven in an houre;

The reverses of fortune God inflicts on his plants - his followers - are shattering in their sudden contrasts: killing and quickening - dying and living.

> Making a chiming of a passing-bell

(A passing bell is a single bell, as used for a funeral, and a chiming is many bells more cheerfully sounding together, as for a wedding.)

> We say amiss
> This or that is:
> The word is all, if we could spell.

We cannot say for certain what will come next; God ordains it, and we are not capable of foretelling - of spelling out for ourselves - what will happen.

In Verse Four he expresses his frustration at being powerless to decide his own fate:

> O that I once past changing were,
> Fast in thy Paradise, where no flower can wither!
> Many a spring I shoot up fair,
> Offring at heav'n, growing and groning thither:
> Nor doth my flower
> Want a spring- showre,
> My sinnes and I joining together.

'Offring at' means 'aiming at'. He is striving towards heaven, not needing God's help. 'Growing and groning' - how he loves playing with similar -sounding words. The flaw here is that he is carrying his sins up with him, and he will have to pay for this in the next verse.

Verse Five:

> But while I grow in a straight line,
> Still upwards bent, as if heav'n were mine own,
> Thy anger comes, and I decline :
> What frost to that ? what pole is not the zone,
> Where all things burn,
> When thou dost turn,
> And the least frown of thine is shown ?

'Bent' means directed or pointed towards. He is naively thinking that he can approach heaven just as he is, sin and all, and he is icily

191

rebuffed. God's anger is like frost, blighting and withering the plant again. And what frost is colder than God's anger? His anger is so frosty that it makes even the cold poles seem warm by comparison - God's slightest frown is far more chilling than the South or North Pole.

After this rebuff comes the wonderful sixth verse. T.S.Eliot in his study of Herbert quotes A.Alvarez, who writes in 'The school of Donne' (published in 1961 by Chatto and Windus):

> 'This is, I suppose, the most perfect and most vivid stanza in the whole of Herbert's work. But it is, in every sense, so natural that its originality is easily missed.'

And Eliot himself says of the verse:

> I cannot resist the thought that in this stanza - itself a miracle of phrasing - the imagery, so apposite to express the achievement of faith which it records, is taken from the experience of the man of delicate physical health who has known much illness.'

Verse Six:

> And now in age I bud again,
> After so many deaths I live and write ;
> I once more smell the dew and rain,
> And relish versing

It is as if he has lived through several lifetimes, which have aged him: God's anger has been like a series of deaths to him, but he has revived and lives again: his senses are so alert that he can even smell the dew; and he is alive enough to take up his pen and write poetry again. Then come the wonderful lines:

> O my only light
> It cannot be
> That I am he
> On whom thy tempests fell all night.

He has God's light - the only light that matters to him - shining on him again, and in the relief of this he can hardly remember the agonies he suffered in the darkness of the black night of God's anger, when he was submerged by the tempests of God's rage. Such simplicity of language goes straight to our deepest awareness.

The first line of the last verse is almost an echo of the first line of Verse three:

> 'These are thy wonders, Lord of *power*' - but in the seventh verse the power is changed to Lord of love. Herbert is basking again in God's approval, but he is aware now that this happiness depends on his own attitude: if he shows arrogance or pride, as he did when in Verse five he said 'as if heav'n were mine own', he will forfeit heaven.

Verse Seven.

> These are thy wonders, Lord of love,
> To make us see we are but flowers that glide :
> Which when we once can finde and prove,
> Thou hast a garden for us, where to bide.
> Who would be more,
> Swelling through store,
> Forfeit their Paradise by their pride.

Never take God's approval for granted, and remember, the attitude God likes best is humility. 'Flowers that glide' has a sense of liquidity about it: rooted flowers don't glide. Whatever the underlying meaning, the image is of impermanence - gliding is not staying still, and to bide often means to stay, or wait, for a while only. Remember, he is saying, you are in this garden of Paradise on sufferance - and if you think you deserve to be there, and are swelled with pride, you may suddenly discover you have forfeited your happy existence in the heavenly garden, and may be thrust out, like Adam and Eve from Eden.

G.E.Veith in his book 'Reformation Spirituality' quotes Cranmer when discussing this poem

'God may hide himself. His purposes may be inscrutable, and they may work at cross-purposes to the human will, but His design, in the words of Cranmer, is to "show himself to be the God of his people, when He seems to have altogether forsaken them; then raising them up when they think he is bringing them down and laying them low; then glorifying them when He is thought to be confounding them; then quickening them when He is thought to be destroying them." God's actions are thus certain to be misinterpreted; their purpose, however violent the means, is sanctification - raising up, glorifying, quickening.'

What Veith, and Cranmer, and Herbert in 'The Flower' are all saying, is that while God may appear to be capricious, there is, behind his inscrutable actions, a sublime purpose, and in order to become part of this we must allow ourselves to acquiesce to whatever he decrees with unquestioning humility. This is perhaps the hardest lesson that Herbert had to learn in his long pilgrimage towards God.

Heaven

O Who will show me those delights on high?
               Echo.   I.
Thou Echo, thou art mortal, all men know.
               Echo.   No.
Wert thou not born among the trees and leaves?
               Echo.   Leaves.
And are there any leaves, that still abide?
               Echo.   Bide.
What leaves are they? Impart the matter wholly.
               Echo.   Holy.
Are holy leaves the Echo then of blisse?
               Echo.   Yes.
Then tell me, what is that supreme delight?
               Echo.   Light.
Light to the minde: what shall the will enjoy?
               Echo.   Joy.
But are there cares and business with the pleasure?
               Echo.   Leisure.
Light, joy and leisure; but shall they persever?
               Echo.   Ever.

Heaven

Heaven is an echo poem. Echo poems were found in literature long before Herbert used the form. Sir Philip Sidney (a relation by marriage to the Pembroke family) has one much less fine than Herbert's, in The Arcadia. Lord Herbert of Cherbury, George's oldest brother, also wrote one. In classical literature Tasso used the form. Monteverdi set one to music in his Vespers. Helen Vendler quotes one by Lord Sterling, written in 1604. She says of Herbert's 'Heaven' that 'it transcends not only all its native predecessors but also its descendants.' She goes on: 'Perhaps it triumphs first for its brevity. And there is a reason for, or depth to, nearly all the rhymes.' She analyses the poem in great depth for seven pages of her book 'The Poetry of George Herbert' (pp.222 -229). She reminds us that in both collections of his poems he put this one just before the sublime last poem, Love(III) - as being worthy of that place. Because of this, and because of its unique form, I have included it in this small anthology of his most remarkable poems. And it is a good example of Herbert's use of words with more than one meaning.

Veith says of it 'That the poem is about the Bible is not immediately obvious', but he does believe that 'Echo' stands for the holy scriptures, and I agree with that interpretation.

O Who will show me those delights on high?
Echo.   I.
Thou Echo, thou art mortal, all men know.
Echo.   No.

The questioner wants to be given a vision of heaven. Echo agrees to do so. But the poet then questions Echo's ability to do this. Everyone knows that Echo's voice stems from copying mortal speech, so must have limited powers. But Echo calmly disagrees - her powers are divine. (Echo was always feminine in classical literature, but Herbert does not give her either sex. For him she is personifying holy scripture, which is divinely inspired.)

Wert thou not born among the trees and leaves?
Echo.   Leaves.

In Greek mythology Echo was a nymph of the mountains who fell in love with Narcissus, and faded away from unrequited love until she was only a disembodied voice. Herbert takes her from that arcadian setting, and relates her to the leaves that are pages of the bible.

> And are there any leaves, that still abide?
> > *Echo.*   Bide.

Vendler asks whether Herbert was aware that the word 'bide' is related to the Latin word 'fidere' - to trust - and also to the Greek word 'paithesthai' - to believe-. Being well versed in classics he surely was, and this small word thus held for him the meaning 'remain in trusting belief'. He is asking if the leaves of the Bible have lasting significance, and Echo answers that their worth, through trust and belief, will last continually.

> What leaves are they? Impart the matter wholly.
> > *Echo.*   Holy.
> Are holy leaves the Echo then of blisse?
> > *Echo.*   Yes.

Vendler asks: 'did he mean 'blisse' to summon up 'blesse'?' Certainly 'yes' rhymes better with bless than with bliss, and this is the least well-matched of his rhymes. He has assured himself that the Bible is a source of bliss, and the soft sibilance of the 'yes' brings this first part of the poem to a moment of pausing on a happy certainty. But there are more questions to come, back to the subject of heaven.

> Then tell me, what is that supreme delight?
> > *Echo.*   Light.
> Light to the minde: what shall the will enjoy?
> > *Echo.*   Joy.
> But are there cares and business with the pleasure?
> > *Echo.*   Leisure.
> Light, joy and leisure; but shall they persever?
> > *Echo.*   Ever.

In the first line of the poem, he asked to know the delights of heaven. Now he asks again, having assured himself that Echo will know the answer. Light shines out from the Bible. Christ's words - 'I am the light of the world' are there. And light - enlightenment - is there for us in heaven. What shall our will -our effort and determination - bring us? They will bring us joy. But is this joy going also to involve much care and hard work ? The answer 'leisure' means that it will bring rest and peace. Herbert is left at the end with these three virtues: light, joy and leisure - these are the delights, he is assured, waiting for him in heaven. And to the final question whether they will always be there, comes the final word 'ever'. Mahler ended 'Das Lied von der Erde' with that word, and at the end of this poem it reverberates in our minds in the same way: a perfect ending. His uncertainties are finally resolved in this last word.

Echo's voice always brings calm and certainty, throughout the poem. Vendler summarises the last lines: 'Surely the doctrine of final perseverance, by which transient grace turns to permanent glory, deserves to have the word 'ever' embodied in it.'

This poem, like 'The Call', shows Herbert's brilliance in using the most restrictive possible poetic structure to express enduring truths.

Love (III)

Love bade me welcome: yet my soul drew back,
        Guiltie of dust and sinne.
But quick-ey'd love, observing me grow slack
        From my first entrance in,
Drew nearer to me, sweetly questioning,
        If I lack'd anything.

A guest, I answer'd, worthy to be here:
        Love said, You shall be he.
I the unkinde, ungratefull? Ah my deare,
        I cannot look on thee.
Love took my hand, and smiling did reply,
        Who made the eyes but I?

Truth, Lord, but I have marr'd them : let my shame
        Go where it doth deserve.
And know you not, sayes Love, who bore the blame?
        My deare, then I will serve.
You must sit down, sayes Love, and taste my meat:
        So I did sit and eat.

Love (lll) By George Herbert

The poem is called Love (lll) because Herbert had already written two other poems called 'Love'. It is perhaps the best known and best loved of all Herbert's poems, apart from the three or four that are often sung as hymns. It has been set to music, by Vaughan Williams. I have heard it read at a wedding. It is the last poem in The Temple, but not necessarily the last he wrote, because it appears in the earlier collection known as the Williams collection. But it has, in its last line, the realisation that no more need be said. It seems a summation of Herbert's troubled life.

The brilliant young philosopher Simone Weil, who died in 1943 aged 34, became a Christian mystic through this poem. 'It became her custom to recite (this poem) about the soul's encounter with Christ; and, as she confided in a Dominican priest, Father Perrin, it was during one such recitation that "Christ himself came down and took possession of me. In my arguments about the insolubility of God I had never foreseen the possibility of that, of a real contact, person to person, here below, between a human being and God."   (Quoted from 'Jesus" by A.N.Wilson. pub. Flamingo 1993.)

The poem is written in three verses with six lines each, alternately long and short, and the rhyme scheme is ABABCC. The scene is that of Christ's parable of the great feast to which none of the originally invited guests come, and people are brought in at the last minute from the streets and lanes .Herbert is picturing himself as one of these latecomers. The parable appears in St. Luke's gospel, chapter 14. Just before the parable comes Christ's well-known advice to an invited guest, and this plays some part too in the poem:

> V.10. When thou art bidden, go and sit down in the lowest room; that when he that bade thee cometh, he may say unto thee, Friend, go up higher: then shalt thou have worship in the presesnce of them that sit at meat with thee.

> V.11. For whosoever exalteth himself shall be abased; and he that humbleth himself shall be exalted.

Then the parable starts at verse 16. 'A certain man made a great supper, and bade many.' They all make excuses as to why they can't come. So the parable continues, at verse 21:

'Go out quickly into the streets and lanes of the city, and bring in hither the poor, and the maimed, and the halt and the blind.' He tells them to 'compel them to come in', 'for I say unto you, that none of those men which were bidden shall taste of my supper.'

Herbert is bidden to a great supper, by Love. Love is his master, Jesus Christ. Herbert himself is one of the halt maimed and blind, brought in from the dusty lanes and totally unfitted for a grand feast. The poem begins

> Love bade me welcome: yet my soul drew back,
>   Guiltie of dust and sinne.

Quick-eyed love, watching carefully and seeing his hesitation, goes up to him and asks him why he is hesitating, and what he needs.

> But quick-ey'd love, observing me grow slack
>   From my first entrance in,
> Drew nearer to me, sweetly questioning,
>   If I lack'd anything.

In his poem 'The Glance' Herbert speaks of 'full-ey'd love', and here he says 'quick ey'd love.' He has great awareness of Christ's eyes, attentive, sensitive, overflowing with love, always directed on him. He uses the adverb 'sweetly': he often gives Christ the quality of sweetness. In 'The Glance' he speaks in the first line of Christ's 'sweet and gracious eye' and, more vividly in the same poem, of 'the sugar'd, strange delight' he felt when he first knew this look to be fixed on him in his youth, when he was 'weltering in sinne.' Sweetness is what invades him from Christ's loving attention.

The second verse has his answer to his lord's questioning about his needs:

> A guest, I answer'd, worthy to be here:

This line has echoes of the prayer from the Church of England Holy Communion service, which Herbert would have known:

> '...and though we be unworthy so much as to gather up the crumbs from under thy table, yet thou art the same lord, whose property is always to have mercy.'

His lord quietly reassures him that he is wanted:

> Love said, You shall be he.
> I the unkinde, ungratefull? Ah my deare,
> I cannot look on thee.
> Love took my hand, and smiling did reply,
> Who made the eyes but I?

Love has now become in the poem the maker of heaven and earth and of every part of mankind: he is responsible for the person that stands so humbly hesitating before him .

The last verse begins with more abject humility and hesitation:

> Truth, Lord, but I have marr'd them : let my shame
> Go where it doth deserve.

But now love becomes Christ himself, who died on the cross to redeem sinners. He does not disagree about Herbert's unworthiness, but tells him that his sins have already been atoned for.

> And know you not, sayes Love, who bore the blame?

Still Herbert does not feel he should be allowed to join the feast, unless he may do so as one of the servants.

> My deare, then I will serve.

Even though he knows himself so far beneath his lord, he twice addresses him in the poem as 'My deare', a term of endearment between two same-level friends. 'My deare' is intimately conversational. and lets us see these two standing together at the door of the banqueting hall, one hesitant with downcast eyes, the other warmly persuasive, drawing him in. And Herbert finally accepts the invitation.

> You must sit down, sayes Love, and taste my meat:
> So I did sit and eat.

One of the simplest lines in English poetry ends the poem and the collection of Herbert's Temple. No word is longer than three letters, and the stress falls on each word equally;

> v v v   v   v   v
> So I did sit and eat.

How careful is the choice of those six words. What if he had said

> 'So I sat down and ate.'

It would be humdrum, everyday and ordinary. Herbert's line has a continuity about it. We have no idea how long he is going to be there - it could be for ever - and the two actions of sitting and eating are simultaneous, not first one, then the next. They are happening together perhaps to the end of time. He shows, in those six words, that in spite of all self-doubts and feelings of unworthiness, he has realised that he is loved, and is to be allowed to inherit the kingdom of heaven, where he will remain in perpetuity.

In our consciousness as we read the poem are the words Christ spoke at the Last Supper to his disciples.. 'Take, eat; this is my body.' (Matthew Chapter 26 Verse 26.) The last sixteen one- syllable words of the poem could be a paraphrase of Christ's own words, when he broke the bread in the upper room.

All through The Temple Herbert doubts his worthiness to be accepted - even though, with Calvin, he believed that ultimately he is one of the elect who is due to be saved. He never once talks of hell-fire or damnation, as Donne does. At the same time, his course towards God has been desperately hard, and he has often resented this, and often doubted therefore that he truly has God's love. But this final poem resolves for ever all his conflicts,which is one reason why for us it is so profoundly moving.

Herbert ended the note that he wrote on his death bed to Nicholas Ferrar, with a copy of The Temple, with these words: he told him that in the poems he would find

> a picture of the many spiritual Conflicts that have past betwixt God and my Soul, before I could subject mine to the will of Jesus my Master, in whose service I have now found perfect freedom.

Love (lll) exemplifies this ultimate peace of mind that Herbert achieved just before he died.

Group Seven
SINGLE LONG POEM (THE SACRIFICE).

The Sacrifice is possibly the most heart-rendingly passionate of all Herbert's poems. In it he imagines himself speaking as Christ at the time of his betrayal, arrest, trial, and crucifixion. The grief and pain he manages to convey are amplified by the desolate refrain to each of the 63 verses except two. 'Was ever grief like mine?' The two, including the last verse, affirm the realisation by Christ that 'Never was grief like mine.'

The Sacrifice

1.   *Oh all ye, who passe by,* whose eyes and minde
To worldly things are sharp, but to me blinde,
To me, who took eyes that I might you finde:
                          Was ever grief like mine?

2.   The Princes of my people make a head
Against their Maker: they do wish me dead,
Who cannot wish, except I give them bread:
                          Was ever grief like mine?

3.   Without me each one, who doth now me brave,
Had to this day been an Egyptian slave.
They use that power against me, which I gave:
                          Was ever grief like mine?

4.   Mine own apostle, who the bag did beare,
Though he had all I had, did not forbeare
To sell me also, and to put me there:
                          Was ever grief like mine?

5.   For thirtie pence he did my death devise,
Who at three hundred did the ointment prize,
Not half so sweet as my sweet sacrifice:
                          Was ever grief like mine?

6.   Therefore my soul melts, and my hearts deare treasure
Drops bloud (the onely beads) my words to measure:
O let this cup passe, if it be thy pleasure:
                          Was ever grief like mine?

7.   These drops being tempered with a sinner's tears
A Balsome are for both the Hemispheres:
Curing all wounds, but mine; all, but my fears:
                          Was ever grief like mine?

8   Yet my disciples sleep: I cannot gain
            One houre of watching; but their drowsie brain
            Comforts not me, and doth my doctrine staine:
                          Was ever grief like mine?

9   Arise, arise, they come. Look how they runne!
            Alas! what haste they make to be undone!
            How with their lanterns do they seek the sunne!
                          Was ever grief like mine?

10.   With clubs and staves they seek me, as a thief,
            Who am the Way and Truth, the true relief;
            Most true to those, who are my greatest grief:
                          Was ever grief like mine?

            11.   *Judas,* dost thou betray me with a kisse?
            Canst thou finde hell about my lippes? and misse
            Of life, just at the gates of life and blisse?
                          Was ever grief like mine?

12.   See, they lay hold on me, not with the hands
            Of faith, but furie: yet at their commands
            I suffer binding, who have loos'd their bands:
                          Was ever grief like mine?

13.   All my Disciples flie; fear puts a barre
            Betwixt my friends and me. They leave the starre,
            That brought the wise men of the East from farre.
                          Was ever grief like mine?

14.   Then from one ruler to another bound
            They leade me; urging, that it was not sound
            What I taught: Comments would the text confound.
                          Was ever grief like mine?

15.   The Priest and rulers all false witnesse seek
    'Gainst him, who seeks not life, but is the meek
    And readie Paschal Lambe of this great week:
                 Was ever grief like mine?

16.   Then they accuse me of great blasphemie,
    That I did thrust into the Deitie,
    Who never thought that any robberie:
                 Was ever grief like mine?

17.   Some said, that I the Temple to the floore
    In three days raz'd, and raised as before.
    Why, he that built the world can do much more:
                 Was ever grief like mine?

18.   Then they condemne me all with that same breath,
    Which I do give them daily, unto death.
    Thus *Adam* my first breathing rendereth.
                 Was ever grief like mine?

19.   They binde, and leade me unto *Herod,* he
    Sends me to *Pilate.* This makes them agree;
    But yet their friendship is my enmitie:
                 Was ever grief like mine?

20.   *Herod* and all his bands do set me light,
    Who teach all hands to warre, fingers to fight,
    And onely am the Lord of Hosts and might:
                 Was ever grief like mine?

21.   *Herod* in judgement sits, while I do stand;
    Examines me with a censorious hand:
    I him obey, who all things else command:
                 Was ever grief like mine?

22.   The *Jews* accuse me with despitefulnesse;
                And vying malice with my gentlenesse,
                Pick quarrels with their onely happinesse:
                            Was ever grief like mine?

23.   I answer nothing, but with patience prove
                If stonie hearts will melt with gentle love.
                But who does hawk at eagles with a dove?
                            Was ever grief like mine?

24.   My silence rather doth augment their crie;
                My dove doth back into my bosome flie,
                Because the raging waters still are high:
                            Was ever grief like mine?

25.   Heark how they crie aloud still, *Crucifie:*
                It is not fir he live a day, they crie,
                Who cannot live lesse than eternally:
                            Was ever grief like mine?

26.   *Pilate,* a stranger, holdeth off; but they,
                Mine owne deare people, cry, *Away, away,*
                With noises confused frighting the day:
                            Was ever grief like mine?

27.   Yet still they shout, and crie, and stop their eares,
                 Putting my life among their sinnes and fears,
                And therefore wish *my blood on them and theirs:*
                            Was ever grief like mine?

28.   See how spite cankers things. These words aright
                Used, and wished, are the whole worlds light:
                But hony is their gall, brightnesse their night:
                            Was ever grief like mine?

29.   They choose a murderer, and all agree
      In him to do themselves a courtesie:
      For it was their own case who killed me:
                        Was ever grief like mine?

30.   And a seditious murderer he was:
      But I the Prince of peace; peace that doth passe
      All understanding, more than heav'n doth glasse:
                        Was ever grief like mine?

31.   Why, Caesar is their onely King, not I:
      He clave the stonie rock, when they were drie;
      But surely not their hearts, as I well trie:
                        Was ever grief like mine?

32.   Ah! how they scourge me! yet my tendernesse
      Doubles each lash: and yet their bitternesse
      Windes up my grief to a mysteriousnesse:
                        Was ever grief like mine?

33.   They buffet him, and box him as they list,
      Who grasps the earth and heaven with his fist,
      And never yet, whom he would punish, miss'd:
                        Was ever grief like mine?

34.   Behold, thet spit on me in scornful wise,
      Who by my spittle gave the blind man eies,
      Leaving his blindnesse to my enemies:
                        Was ever grief like mine?

35.   My face they cover, though it be divine.
      As *Moses* face was vailed, so is mine,
      Lest on their double-dark souls either shine:
                        Was ever grief like mine?

36.   Servants and abjects flout me; they are wittie:
           Now prophesie who stikes thee, is their dittie.
           So they in me deny all pitie:
                         Was ever grief like mine?

37.   And now I am deliver'd unto death,
           Which each one calls for so with utmost breath,
           That he before me well nigh suffereth:
                         Was ever grief like mine?

38.   Weep not, deare friends, since I for both have wept
           When all my tears were bloud, the while you slept:
           Your tears for your own fortunes should be kept:
                         Was ever grief like mine?

39.   The souldiers lead me to the Common Hall;
           There they deride me, they abuse me all:
           Yet for twelve heavenly legions I could call:
                         Was ever grief like mine?

40.   Then with a scarlet robe they me aray;
           Which shows my bloud to be the onely way
           And cordiall left to repair mans decay:
                         Was ever grief like mine?

41.   Then on my head a crown of thorns I wear:
           For these are all the grapes *Sion* doth bear,
           Though I my vine planted and watred there:
                         Was ever grief like mine?

42.   So sits the earths great curse in *Adams* fall
           Upon my head: so I remove it all
           From th' earth unto my brows, and bear the thrall:
                         Was ever grief like mine?

44.   They bow their knees to me, and cry, *Hail king:*
          What ever scoffes and scornfulnesse can bring,
          I am the floore, the sink, where it they fling:
                    Was ever grief like mine?

45.   Yet since mans scepters are as frail as reeds,
          And thorny sll their crowns, bloudie their weeds,
          I, who am Truth, turn into truth their deeds:
                    Was ever grief like mine?

46.   The souldiers also spit upon that face,
          Which angels did desire to have the grace,
          And prophets, once to see, but found no place:
                    Was ever grief like mine?

47.   Thus trimmed, forth they bring me to the rout,
          Who *Crucifie him,* crie with one strong shout.
          God holds his peace at man, and man cries out:
                    Was ever grief like mine?

48.   They leade me in once more, and putting then
          Mine own clothes on, they leade me out agen.
          Whom devils flie, thus is he toss'd of men:
                    Was ever grief like mine?

49.   And now wearie of sport, glad to ingrosse
          All spite in one, counting my life their losse,
          They carrie me to my most bitter crosse:
                    Was ever grief like mine?

50.   My crosse I bear my self, untill I faint:
          Then Simon bears it for me by constraint,
          The decreed burden of each mortall saint:
                    Was ever grief like mine?

51.   *O all ye who passe by, behold and see;*
        Man stole the fruit, but I must climbe the tree;
        The tree of life to all, but onely me:
                Was ever grief like mine?

52.   Lo, here I hang, charg'd with a world of sinne,
        The greater world o' th' two; for that came in
        By words, but this by sorrow I must win:
                Was ever grief like mine?

53.   Such sorrow as, if sinfull man could feel,
        Or feel his part, he would not cease to kneel,
        Till all were melted, though he were all steel:
                Was ever grief like mine?

54.   But, *O my God, my God!* why leav'st thou me,
        The sonne, in whom thou dost delight to be?
        My God, my God ------
                Never was grief like mine.

55.   Shame tears my soul, my bodie many a wound;
        Sharp nails pierce this, but sharper that confound;
        Reproches, which are free, while I am bound.
                Was ever grief like mine?

56.   *Now heal thyself, Physician; now come down.*
        Alas! I did so, when I left my crown
        And fathers smile for you, to feel his frown:
                Was ever grief like mine?

57.   In healing not myself, there doth consist
        All that salvation, which ye now resist;
        Your safety in my sicknesse doth subsist:
                Was ever grief like mine?

58.   Betwixt two theeves I spend my utmost breath,
As he that for some robberie suffereth.
Alas! What have I stollen from you? Death.
                Was ever grief like mine?

59.   A king my title is, prefixt on high;
Yet by my subjects am condemn'd to die
A servile death in servile companie:
                Was ever grief like mine?

60.   They give me vinegar mingled with gall
But more with malice: yet, when they did call,
With Manna, Angels food, I fed them all:
                Was ever grief like mine?

61.   They part my garments, and by lot dispose
My coat, the type of love, which once cur'd those
Who sought for help, never malicious foes:
                Was ever grief like mine?

62.   Nay, after death their spite shall further go;
For they will pierce my side, I full well know;
That as sinne came, so Sacraments might flow:
                Was ever grief like mine?

63.   But now I die; now all is finished.
My wo, mans weal: and now I bow my head.
Onely let others say, when I am dead,
                Never was grief like mine.

The Sacrifice

W.H.Auden considered The Sacrifice to be Herbert's greatest poem. (A Kind of Poetic Justice: Observer Review, Oct. 29th 1972, p.38.) William Empson, in Seven Types of Ambiguity, says of the poem that in it is 'a magnificence (Herbert) never excelled.' But not all his critics agree. Helen Vendler, in her book 'The Poetry of George Herbert' writes: 'Though no-one can deny the finished elegance of The Sacrifice, it is not, in spite of its subject, one of Herbert's immediately moving poems.' She talks of its 'frigid ingenuity and stylisation.'

Another - and perhaps the most helpful critic, Rosamund Tuve, in her book 'A Reading of George Herbert' - extols the poem for many pages. Her aim is to tell us the influences that inspired Herbert to write this poem in the way that he did. She tells us that this particular style of poem: the monologue spoken by Christ; the symbolically used Old Testament refrain; the special mingling of contradictory emotions in the speaker, and the general poetic tone of the whole, were traditional for many generations before Herbert used them.

'All the types of ironic contrast, upon which Herbert's poem is constructed and which work down into its details to give it that ambiguity, density, and ambivalence of tone that we think of as so specially 'metaphysical' are explicit in the tradition of mediaeval thought. How like' she says 'metaphysical wit is to mediaeval habits of mind.'

Armed with these contradictory and enlightening criticisms, it is necessary to make up our own minds. There are 63 verses to the poem: each has four lines; the first three have a mutual rhyme; the fourth in every verse except two, is the same tragic question;

Was ever grief like mine?

Herbert never used this form again. The poem is Christ himself speaking, describing his own betrayal, passion, and crucifixion, and the final refrain to each verse adds such poignancy that it is like one long lamentation of agony.

The first verse takes its opening words from the Lamentations of Jeremiah over the city of Jerusalem, and also from verse 39 of Chapter 27 of St. Matthew's gospel, where he says of the people watching Christ's crucifixion:'And they that passed by reviled him, wagging their heads.'

Verse 1.

> Oh all ye, who passe by, whose eyes and minde
> To worldly thing are sharp, but to me blinde,
> To me, who took eyes that I might thee finde:
> > Was ever grief like mine?

He took on flesh and blood, and therefore eyes, in order to know at first hand the human situation, and help mankind.

In verse 8, he is speaking from the Garden of Gethsemane:

Verse 8.

> Yet my disciples sleep, I cannot gain
> One hour of watching; but their drowsy brain
> Comforts not me, and doth my doctrine stain:
> > Was ever grief like mine?

The description of his betrayal goes on in the present tense, making us feel we are there with him as they come to arrest him in the garden:

Verse 10.

> With clubs and staves they seek me, as a thief,
> Who am the Way and Truth, the true relief,
> Most true to those, who are my greatest grief:
> > Was ever grief like mine?

In verse 13, as he does in so many other verses, he combines two different bible stories:

Verse 13.

> All my disciples flie; fear puts a barre
> Betwixt my friends and me. They leave the starre
> That brought the wise men of the East from farre.
> > Was ever grief like mine?

Verse 17 has a deliberate pun: something Herbert often did, as did his friend John Donne: Empson says of this verse: 'He is speaking with pathetic simplicity, and an innocent surprise that people should treat him so.'

Verse 17.

> Some said, that I the Temple to the floore
> In three days raz'd, and raised as before,
> Why, he that built the world can do much more:
>   Was ever grief like mine?

Verses 23 and 24 describe Christ's questioning by the High Priests and Elders, and Herbert uses the metaphor of hawking; pursuing an eagle with such an inappropriate bird as a dove. Then in verse 24 he brings into the trial scene the story of Noah sending the dove from the ark to find dry land:

Verse 23.

> I answer nothing, but with patience prove
> If stonie hearts will melt with gentle love.
> But who does hawk at eagles with a dove?
>   Was ever grief like mine?

Verse 24.

> My silence rather doth augment their crie;
> My dove does back into my bosom flie,
> Because the raging waters still are high:
>   Was ever grief like mine?

The next verse is more dramatic: Christ shows the paradox of the people condemning to death an immortal being:

Verse25.

> Heark how they crie aloud still, Crucifie:
> It is not fit he live a day, they crie,
> Who cannot live lesse than eternally:
>   Was ever grief like mine?

Verse 51 caused a controversy between the two scholars William Empson and Rosamund Tuve. This is the verse:

Verse 51.

> O all ye who passe by, behold and see;
> Man stole the fruite, but I must climb the tree;
> The tree of life to all, but only me,
>> Was ever grief like mine?

(The first line is the full quotation from the Lamentations of Jeremiah.)

Empson wrote in his Seven Types of Ambiguity (page 232) that Herbert meant that Christ was climbing the apple tree in the garden of Eden, in order to put back the apple that Adam and Eve ate, and that Christ himself had done the stealing. Tuve completely refutes this theory, and explains at some length in her book 'A Reading of George Herbert' (pages 81 -91) that mediaeval tradition linked the tree in the Garden of Eden to the cross on which Christ was crucified. This explanation is born out by reading one of Herbert's Latin poems, (Passio Discerpta no.XII): a translation of which goes:

> Zaccheus, that he might see you,
> Climbed a tree: now you yourself
> Climb up, so that, the work turned round,
> Ease may be stored up for us,
> And sweat for you.

Each verse has a stark contradiction and compelling paradox: it is this which gives the poem its power: each verse is a shock, a striking opposition, a gasp of realisation. To me there is a sense of Christ's passive outrage at such betrayal and total misunderstanding; and there is heartbreak: one's throat is caught, through the rhythm, by a feeling of sobbing- the grief of the poem is palpable - the indignation becomes ours as we read the injustice of each verse. The most poignant of all is verse 54:

Verse 54.

> But O my God, my God! Why leav'st thou me,
> The Sonne, in whom thou dost delight to be?
> My God, my God ----
> Never was grief like mine.

The refrain changes for the first time. Herbert can be imagined being unable to finish that verse, for the emotion he is feeling. A true cry of greatest agony. Herbert re-lives, for himself and for us, stage by stage, the betrayal and death of Christ.By entering in to Christ's mind, and speaking through him as he experiences the Passion, he allows us to feel the cruel injustice of his desertion by his disciples and his treatment by the people of Jerusalem. The poem jolts us with each verse into a realisation of what Christ had to endure. And we get a knowledge of Herbert's commitment to the truth of the New Testament account of Christ's Passion, and of his commitment to Christ, and his love for him, and of his certainty that Christ was the son of God, who died to propitiate our sins.

The last verse ends the poem on a note of utter resignation.

Verse 63.

> But now I die: now all is finished.
> My wo, man's weal: and now I bow my head.
> Only let others say, when I am dead,
> Never was grief like mine.

To me it is a great, well-sustained, deeply felt and most moving poem. Its mediaeval counterparts with which Rosamund Tuve is familiar, are not easily available to us. This Renaissance inheritor of theirs is wholly accessible, and even has a feeling of modernity in some of its use of language. It is, as Auden and Empson said, Herbert at his best.

SELECT BIBLIOGRAPHY

ANDREWES, Lancelot. Two Answers. Oxford
    University Press. 1854.

AUBREY, John. Brief Lives.

BENNETT, Joan. Five Metaphysical Poets.
    Cambridge University Press. 1964

BLACKBURN, Simon. Think. Oxford University Press.1999.

BLACKSTONE, Bernard. The Ferrar Papers.
    Cambridge University Press. 1938.

BLYTHE, Ronald. A Priest to the Temple or The Country Parson.
    Edited, with introduction. Canterbury Press. Norwich,2003.

BLYTHE, Ronald. Divine Landscapes.

BRADBROOK, Muriel C. Writers and their Work:
    T.S. Eliot. Faber and Faber, 1967.

BROWNE, Deborah A., Ph D. Christianity in the 21st Century.
    Specific chapter: Creation Spirituality by Matthew
    Fox. Crossroads Publishing Co., New York, 1981.

CHARLES, A.M. Facsimile of Bodleian manuscript of
    George Herbert's Poems. Delmar, New York, 1979.

CHARLES, Amy M. A Life of George Herbert.
    Cornell University Press, 1977.

CLARKE, Elizabeth. Theory and Theology in George
    Herbert's Poetry. Clarendon, Oxford,1997.

ELIOT, Thomas Stearns. George Herbert. (Edited by
     Peter Porter.) Northcote House,1994.

ELIOT Thomas Stearns. Four Quartets. Faber, London, 1963.

EMPSON, William. Seven Types of Ambiguity.
     Chatto and Windus,, 1973.

GARDNER Helen. The Composition of the Four
     Quartets. Faber, London1963.

GRIERSON, Hubert.J.C. Metaphysical Poetry from Donne
     to Butler. Oxford University Press, 1921.

GYSI, Lydia (Mother Maria). George Herbert: Aspects of his
     Theology. Lovat Press, Newport Pagnell,1972.

HEANEY, Seamus. The Redress of Poetry. Faber, London,1995.

HEDERMAN, Mark Patrick. The Haunted Inkwell.
     The Columba Press, Dublin, 2001.

HODGKINS, Christopher. Authority, Church and Society in George
     Herbert: Return To the Middle Way. New York, 1993.

HUDSON, Roger. London: Portrait of a City. Folio Society,1998.

HUTCHINSON, F.E. The Works of George Herbert.
     Clarendon Press Oxford.1964.

LEEDHAM-GREEN, Elizabeth. A Concise History of the
     University of Cambridge. Cambridge University Press, 1996.

MACCULLOUGH, Diarmaid. Cranmer.
     Yale University Press, 1996.

MACCULLOUGH, Diarmaid. The Later Reformation
     in England -1547 -1603. Macmillan,1990.

MAGEE, Patrick. George Herbert at Bemerton.

MASON, Kenneth. George Herbert, Priest and Poet.
     Sisters of the Love of God Press.1998

MCCLOSKEY, M. and MURPHY, P.R., Translations of
George Herbert from Latin. Athens, Ohio, 1965.

NICOLSON, Adam. Power and Glory: Jacobean England and the
Making of the King James Bible. Harper Collins, 2003.

PAGE, Nick. George Herbert: A Portrait.
Monarch, Tonbridge Wells, 1993.

SHORTHOUSE, Joseph Henry. John Inglesant. 1st pub.
1880. Pub. MacMillan Caravan Library, 1930.

STEWART, Alan. Philip Sidney, A Double Life.
Chatto and Windus, London, 2000.

THOMAS, R.S. A Choice of George Herbert's Verse,
with introduction. Faber, London, 1967.

TOWNSEND, Dorothea. The Life and Letters of Endymion Porter.

TUVE, Rosamund. A Reading of George Herbert.
University of Chicago Press, 1952.

VEITH, Gene Edward Jr. Reformation Spirituality. Lewisburg
Bucknell University Press, London and Associated Press, 1985.

VENDLER, Helen Hennessy. The Poetry of George Herbert.
Harvard University Press, Cambridge, Mass., 1985

WALPOLE, Horace. The Life of Lord Herbert of Cherbury (edited
by Walpole) First Pub. 1764. This edition pub.1826.

WALTON, Izaak. Life of George Herbert, Life of John Donne.

WILLIAMS, Rowan. Anglican Identities. Darton
Longman, Todd, London,2004.

DISTINGUISHED CONTEMPORARIES OF HERBERT'S, OTHER THAN WRITERS.

MONARCHS.

Queen Elizabeth I. …..........…...….......….......…..Reigned 1558-1603
James I and VI of Scotland….......…........…...…..................…..1603 1625.
Charles I….…….…........…..............…....................................1625-1649

ARCHBISHOPS OF CANTERBURY.

John Whitgift…..............…...........…Archbishop of Canterbury 1583-1604
   1530-1604
Richard Bancroft….………........................…......…..............…….....1604-1611
   1544-1611
George Abbott….………....…...............................…...............1611-1633
   1562-1633
William Laud….………....…............…................…...….................1633-1644
   1573-1645

STATESMEN.

Second Earl of Essex…..……......................................…....…..........1566-1601
Sir Thomas Overbury….……....….....................…..................…...1581-1613
John Pym….……...........…...….…..........1584-1643
1st Duke of Buckingham….……....…...................................….........1592-1628
1st Earl of Strafford….……....…...................................….................1593-1641
John Hampden….……....…..….…..........1594-1643
Oliver Cromwell….……....…..…..............1599-1658

THEOLOGIANS AND DIVINES.

Richard Hooker...1554-1600
Lancelot Andrewes...1555-1626
Jacobus Arminius...1560-1609
Nicholas Ferrar...1592-1637

COMPOSERS.

John Taverner c.1495-1545

Thomas Tallis 1505-1585
William Byrd c.1542-1643
Thomas Morley 1557-1623
John Bull 1562-1625
Thomas Campion 1567-1628
John Wilbye 1574-1638
Thomas Weelkes 1575-1623
Philip Rosseter c.1575-1623
Orlando Gibbons 1583-1625.

Giovanni Palestrina c.1525-1594
Claudio Monteverdi 1567-1643

TABLE OF CHRONOLOGY OF
CONTEMPORARY WRITERS TO HERBERT

1552 EDMUND SPENSER------------------------------------1599
1552 Sir Walter Raleigh------------------------------------1618
1553 John Lyly--1606
1554 Sir Philip Sidney------------------------------------1586
1559 George Chapman--------------------------------------1634
1561 SIR FRANCIS BACON----------------------------------1626
1562 Samuel Daniel--1619
1563 Michael Drayton--------------------------------------1631
1564 **WILLIAM SHAKESPEARE**----------------------------1616
1564 Christopher Marlowe ----------------------------------1593
1573 BEN JONSON--1637
1573 JOHN DONNE--1631
1580 Lord Herbert of Cherbury------------------------------1648
c1580 John Webster--------------------------------------c1630
1588 Thomas Hobbes--------------------------------------1679
1591 Robert Herrick--------------------------------------1674
1593 **GEORGE HERBERT**----------------------------------1633
1596 Thomas Carew--------------------------------------1639
1606 Edmund Waller--------------------------------------1687
1608 JOHN MILTON--1674
1609 Sir John Suckling------------------------------------1642
1613 Richard Crashaw------------------------------------1649
1618 Abraham Cowley------------------------------------1667
1618 Richard Lovelace------------------------------------1657
1621 Henry Vaughan--------------------------------------1695
1621 Andrew Marvell--------------------------------------1678
1626 John Aubrey--1697
1628 John Bunyan--1688
1631 John Dryden--1700

APPENDIX

Nicholas Ferrar's introduction to 'The Temple', published with the first edition, Cambridge, 1633.

THE PRINTERS TO THE READER.

The dedication of this work having been made by the authour to the *Divine Majestie* onely,** how should we now presume to interest any mortall man in the patronage of it? Much lesse think we it meet to seek the recommendation of the Muses for that which himself was confident to have been inspired by a diviner breath than flows from *Helicon*. The world therefore shall receive it in that naked simplicitie with which he left it, without any addition either of support or ornament, more than is included in it self. We leave it free and unforestalled to every mans judgment and to the benefit that he shall find by perusall. Onely for the clearing of some passages, we have thought it not unfit to make the common Reader privie to some few particularities of the condition and disposition of the Person;

** The dedication Ferrar refers to is the following short poem which Herbert put at the beginning of The Temple:

The Dedication.

Lord, my first fruits present themselves to thee;
Yet not mine neither: for from thee they came,
And must return. Accept of them and me,
And make us strive, who shall sing best thy name.
Turn their eyes hither, who shall make a gain:
Theirs, who shall hurt themselves or me, refrain.

Being nobly born, and as eminently endued with gifts of the minde, and having by industrie and happy education perfected them to that great height of excellencie, whereof his Fellowship of Trinitie Colledge in Cambridge, and his Orator-ship in the Universitie, together with that knowledge which the Kings Court had taken of him, could make relation farre above ordinarie. Quitting both his deserts and all the opportunities that he had for worldly preferment, he betook himself to the Sanctuarie and Temple of God, choosing rather to serve at Gods Altar than to seek the honour of State-employments. As for those inward enforcements to this course (for outward there was none), which many of these ensuing verses bear witnesse of, they detract not from the freedome, but adde to the honour of this resolution in him. As God had enabled him, so He accounted him meet not onely to be called, but to be compelled to this service; wherein his faithfull discharge was such as may make him justly a companion to the primitive Saints, and a pattern or more for the age he lived in.

To testify his independencie upon all others, and to quicken his diligence in this kinde, he used his ordinary speech when he made mention of the blessed name of our Lord and Saviour, Jesus Christ, to adde, *My Master.*

Next God, he loved that which God himself had magnified above all things - that is, his Word: so as he hath been heard to make some solemn protestation, that he would not part with one leaf thereof for the whole world, if it were offered him in exchange.

His obedience and conformitie to the Church and the discipline thereof was singularly remarkable. Though he abounded in private devotions, yet went he every morning and evening with his familie to the church; and by his example, exhortations, and encouragements, drew the greater part of his parishioners to accompanie him dayly in the publick celebration of Divine Service.

As for worldly matters, his love and esteem of them was so little, as no man can more ambitiously seek than he did earnestly endeavour the resignation of an Ecclesiasticall dignitie, which he was possessour of. But God permitted not the accomplishment of this desire, having ordained him His instrument for reedifying of the church belonging thereunto, that had layen ruinated almost twenty yeares. The reparation whereof, having been ineffectually attempted by publick collections, was in the end by his own and some few others private free-will-offerings SUCCESSFULLY effected. With the remembrance whereof, as of an especiall good work, when a friend went about to comfort him on his deathbed, he made answer, *it is a good work, if it be sprinkled with the bloud of Christ:* otherwise then in this respect he could finde nothing to glorie or comfort himself with, neither in this, nor in any other thing.

And these are but a few of many that might be said, which we have chosen to premise as a glance to some parts of the ensuing book, and for an example to the Reader. We conclude with his own Motto, with which he used to conclude all things that might seem to tend any way to his own honour;

LESSE THEN THE LEAST OF GODS MERCIES.

Printed in the United Kingdom
by Lightning Source UK Ltd.
119088UK00001B/136